CELIBATE LOVING

CELIBATE LOVING

Encounter in Three Dimensions

edited by

MARY ANNE HUDDLESTON, I.H.M.

PAULIST PRESS♦NEW YORK♦RAMSEY

Book design by Maria L. Maggi

Copyright © 1984
by Mary Anne Huddleston

Library of Congress
Catalog Card Number: 83-61996

ISBN: 0-8091-2588-9

Published by Paulist Press
545 Island Road, Ramsey, N.J. 07446

Printed and bound in the
United States of America

Contents

PART THREE
SOCIAL DIMENSIONS OF CELIBACY

Acknowledgments

The editor acknowledges with gratitude the following reprint permissions:

CARROLL, L. PATRICK. Ch. 4. "Becoming a Celibate Lover" from *To Love, To Share, To Serve* by L. Patrick Carroll. © 1979 by the Order of St. Benedict, Collegeville, Minnesota. Reprinted by permission of The Liturgical Press.

CLARK, KEITH. Ch. 7. "Becoming What All People Are" from *An Experience of Celibacy* by Keith Clark. © 1982 by Ave Maria Press, Notre Dame, Indiana. Reprinted by permission of Ave Maria Press.

CONNOLLY, PATRICK J. "A Priest's Thoughts on Celibacy" from "Perspectives," *The Baltimore Sun,* Sunday Supplement (March 2, 1980), K1-2. © 1982 by Patrick J. Connolly. Reprinted by permission of the author.

FINN, VIRGINIA S. "Two Ways of Loving" from *Affectivity and Sexuality: Studies in Jesuit Spirituality,* 10 (March-May, 1978), 109–122. © 1977 by the American Assistancy Seminar on Jesuit Spirituality. Reprinted by permission of the American Assistancy Seminar.

GARVEY, JOHN. "A Married Layman on Celibacy" from *Commonweal,* 106 (October 26, 1979), 585–588. © 1979 by Commonweal Publishing Company. Reprinted by permission of Edward S. Skillin, Publisher.

KAVANAUGH, JOHN F. Ch. 9. "Christ and the Idols of Capitalism" (Tables only.) and "Christian Practice in Personal Form" from *Following Christ in a Consumer Society* by John F. Kavanaugh. © 1981 by Orbis Books, Maryknoll, N.Y. Reprinted by permission of Orbis Books.

KIESLING, CHRISTOPHER. Ch. 10. "Difficulties in Celibate Love" from *Celibacy, Prayer and Friendship* by Christopher Kiesling. © 1978 by the Society of St. Paul. Reprinted by permission of Alba House.

KNIGHT, DAVID. "Will the Church Need Celibates?" from *New Catholic World,* (Vol. 216, No. 1292, Sept./Oct., 1973), 207–211. © by The Missionary Society of St. Paul the Apostle in the State of New York. Used by permission of Paulist Press.

KRAFT, WILLIAM. "Celibate Genitality" from *Review for Religious,* 36 (July, 1977), 600–612. © 1977 By *Review for Religious.* Used by permission of *Review for Religious.*

MITCHELL, KENNETH R. "Priestly Celibacy from a Psychological Perspective" from *The Journal of Pastoral Care,* 24 (December, 1970), 216–226. © 1970 by the Association for Clinical Pastoral Education, Inc. Used by permission of the Association for Clinical Pastoral Education, Inc.

MOORE, SEBASTIAN. "Sex, God and the Church" from *The Inner Loneliness* by Sebastian Moore. © 1982 by Sebastian Moore. Used by permission of The Crossroad Publishing Company.

MURPHY-O'CONNOR, JEROME. ". . . Celibacy and Community" from *What Is Religious Life?* by Jerome Murphy-O'Connor. © 1977 by the author. Reprinted by permission of Michael Glazier, Inc.

NOUWEN, HENRI. Ch. II. "Celibacy and the Holy" from *Clowning in Rome* by Henri J.M. Nouwen. © 1979 by the author. Reprinted by permission of Doubleday and Company, Inc.

PABLE, MARTIN W. "Psychology and Asceticism of Celibacy" from *Review for Religious,* 34 (March, 1975), 266–276. © 1975 by Review for Religious. Reprinted by permission of *Review for Religious.*

Foreword

SEBASTIAN MOORE, O.S.B.

ONE OF THE WORST intellectual vices of our culture is an addiction to binary oppositions, a programming that we are coming to share with our computers. Anyone who promotes anything is taken to be demoting its opposite. In fact, a good promotion of celibacy is a promotion of marriage. The marriage between people looks to the marriage within people. Variety is one of the Spirit's favorite names. I would expect the Age of the Spirit to feature a flowering at once of the married and celibate life. When that old Victorian mystagogue, Thomas Carlyle, said that the Protestant churches, in abandoning celibacy, lost the soul of Europe, it was perhaps to the loss of variety, of socialized spiritual versatility, that he was pointing.

So this anthology seems to be just what we want—not a treatise *on* celibacy but witnesses *to* it, with all the ambiguity and untidiness that this approach entails. I am very happy and honored to be introducing it.

Introduction

MARY ANNE HUDDLESTON, I.H.M.

THERE CAN BE JOY in celibacy. That this is more than fantasy, some celibates give witness. Of course, there are some other celibates: the narcissistic bachelors, the persnickety old maids, the callous and the scrupulous, the drivers and the dilettantes, malingerers and all the rest. Yet in among some maladjusted celibates—not different from their counterparts at-large—are creative, productive, richly human celibate men and women. I know them and have known them.

These men and women are not icebergs: they feel their sexuality within their veins and bones. They are not anti-"sex." They value "sex," but not as a panacea for their problems, because they are not naive. They are aware that far more partners go to bed than ever before, but many of these partners' lives—for all their genital sharing—are unfulfilled. They are aware as well that over one-half of all the marriages today break up almost before they begin, leaving some question about the therapeutic value of genital intimacy in itself.

Nor are these celibates entrapped in celibacy; they know they can escape it by the flick-of-a-will. They do not

3

find their fulfillment *in spite of* celibacy. Instead, they are who they are, in the living out of celibacy for a cause, in ambiguity sometimes, in risk and struggle often, but, whatever else, in love.

With such human celibates as these, either in person or more often through their writings, I have tried to acquaint the seminarians with whom I have worked and whom I have taught. Heartened by the obvious relief and growth and gratitude of these future priests, I began to wonder how I could put persons beyond the seminary boundaries in touch with these very human celibates. Out of my wondering and consultation, this anthology came to be.

Its objective, then, is very simple. It is to offer positive insights which can interrupt the current barrage of negativity toward celibacy. The volume offers these insights to anyone who may be interested, that is, to anyone who can or does believe that celibacy, albeit not for everyone, is valid for some. In particular, the book addresses itself to spiritual formation staffs and to men and women in the process of formation for religious life and/or priesthood.

For the selection of the writings in the book, the rationale is also simple. What appear here are the articles and book chapters which have proved most helpful to me in teaching and in spiritual direction. As will be evident, the writings with one exception originally appeared in print within the last eleven years. Without contrivance, the selections fall easily into three categories: psychological, spiritual, and social dimensions of celibacy. Of necessity, a number of excellent essays have been excluded from the book. By way of compensation, however, the titles of some of these essays appear in the annotated bibliography at the end of the volume. The editor regrets the sexist language in the individual essays.

Although the rationale for the anthology is simple, my initial choice of the writings for use with seminarians was contingent upon multiple presuppositions. I acknowledge that these are not original, and wish to articulate them here.

The first presupposition is the concept of celibacy itself, which, formulated by Christopher Kiesling, is as follows:

> The celibates we are talking about in this book not only are unmarried but also endeavor to forego all directly willful indulgence in pleasures of genital sex, whether with others or alone.[1]

Second, and paradoxically, the devaluation of celibacy so prevalent today is linked somehow to a devaluation of sexuality itself. This devaluation in turn, wrote Paul Ricoeur, stems from the divorce of sexuality from the sacred.[2]

Third, though celibacy is not for everyone, it is also not, *per se,* injurious to bodily health or destructive of the human psyche. Fourth, there is a lack of wisdom in casting celibacy as a scapegoat for all the intrapersonal and interpersonal tensions of clerics and religious. In fact, in this editor's opinion, unless personal agendas other than sexuality are attended to, "genital encounters," whether in or out of marriage, will not alleviate the tensions. It is even

---

1. Christopher Kiesling, O.P., *Celibacy, Prayer and Friendship* (Staten Island: Alba House, 1978), p. xvii.
2. Paul Ricoeur, "Wonder, Eroticism, and Enigma," *Cross Currents,* 14 (Spring, 1964), pp. 133–134.

possible that such encounters will compound the tensions, an hypothesis which any honest married person or therapist could support.

A fifth presupposition: whereas "genital sex" is not for celibates as Kiesling defines them, sexuality most surely is, for sexuality and celibacy are inseparable. Furthermore, if human beings, as I regard them, are relational body persons, they cannot possibly relate a-sexually, though, of course, if they are celibates, they should relate a-genitally. Correlative to the fifth is the sixth presupposition. It is that celibacy should be a way of loving—authentic loving—or that loving which always promotes the autonomy of the other person.[3]

One last observation: too much "sex" like too much anything ends in glutting. Ironically, however, out of the sex-glut of the last decades, there seems to be emerging in America a trend toward *The New Celibacy.* So says Gabrielle Brown in her best seller by this title.[4] Her chapter on "Celibacy for Today's Society" has wisdom from which even experienced celibates can learn. This sample is in point:

> As a society, we've certainly learned that it's okay to be sexual. We've taken up the cause of sexuality and are avoiding repression eagerly. But what has been the result? For one thing, we're *still* obsessed by sex. At least we think it's sex we are always going to be longing for. . . .
>
> Celibacy may be one way to compensate for the overplay of sex. When sexual activity is overvalued, the center of

---

3. Maurice Nedoncelle, *Love and the Person* (New York: Sheed and Ward, 1966), pp. 8, 49.

4. Gabrielle Brown, *The New Celibacy* (New York: Ballantine Books, 1980).

personal growth within the society may be off. . . . Celibacy allows sex to settle back into the fullness of its own nature, to experience its own potential and, subsequently, to reinvest in other channels of communication that we seem to need badly.

For while we've been concentrating on being sexual, we've neglected a lot of other paths of exchange. . . .[5]

And now acknowledgments. Giving thanks is always risky, for so easily can one omit the names of those to whom one really is indebted. Risk notwithstanding, the editor must thank the following for their assistance, tangible and other: her patient relatives; members of her own religious congregation—"Monroe I.H.M.'s"—too numerous to name; the president-rector of St. Mary's Seminary and University (Baltimore) and faculty colleagues past and present; her directees and students, especially those in Developmental Psychology, 1982. For Sebastian Moore's uncommon insights and his graciousness in writing them in the Foreword, I am deeply indebted and honored. The head, heart, and hands of certain other individuals deserve special mention: Joseph Muenzer for a special contribution; Paige Blakely, Michael Sullivan, and Charles Mitchell for help in preparing the manuscript; Mary Jane Brown, I.H.M. and Jesuits Howard Gray and Michael Proterra for their suggestions about the content and format of the book. As forecasted, when I first considered Paulist Press as publisher, its editors, Douglas Fisher in particular, have been efficient and cordial in negotiations.

Finally, I must give thanks to the "inner circle" of friends, single and married, with relatives among them, who have kept alive the flame in my heart. In the warmth

---

5. *Ibid.,* pp. 218–219.

of their love, I have come to realize that all love is gift and mystery. Through the gift and mystery of their friendship, I have come to an experiential understanding of the connection between love and celibacy. Liberated myself by this understanding, I desire that all celibates be free—free to experience the tender love of the Lord, and to mediate it to others. To try to contribute to this liberation is the deep-down reason for this anthology.

PART ONE

PSYCHOLOGICAL DIMENSIONS OF CELIBACY

Psychology and Asceticism
of Celibacy

MARTIN W. PABLE, O.F.M., CAP.

I AM OFTEN ASKED—by priests, seminarians, and religious—what I as a priest-psychologist think about celibacy. My usual response is that I am deeply convinced of the
value of celibacy, both for the Church as a whole and for
myself as an individual priest and religious. But in my ten
years of counseling with priests and religious, I have come
to see the sharp pain and the heavy burden that celibacy
often entails for good men and women in the Church. I
believe it is a gift of God, given to relatively few Christians, and that it is one of the essential foundations of the
religious life. As such, I do not like to see it downgraded,
ridiculed, or lived in an inauthentic manner.

The past ten years have produced a rich literature on
the theology of celibacy in a post-Vatican II framework.
Similarly, formation programs have developed positive,
healthy approaches to training in celibacy. I do not wish to
cover the same ground in this article. What strikes me is
that little has been said in these about the asceticism of celibacy. The other day one of my friends, who is spiritual
director in a seminary, told me he is putting together a

11

modern bibliography on fasting. He said he is having a hard time filling up one page. It is the same way, I think, with asceticism. The notion has fallen on hard times, and it is not fashionable to write about it. But I think it is crucial for understanding celibacy.

THE MEANING OF MORTIFICATION

My starting point will be the beautiful series in the *National Catholic Reporter* by James Carroll during Advent of 1971. The second of that series was entitled "Mortification for Liberation," and there Fr. Carroll made the statement that struck me so forcefully. He said: "Mortification at its best is an act of radical doubt; it is the way to raise questions about what everyone takes for granted. Mortification is the way to question the fundamental assumptions of each age and each institution from this standpoint: do they enable or prevent human life to the full?"[1] Then he went on to list some of the assumptions of our time that mortification calls into question: that consumption of things, pleasures, and experiences makes one happy; to sit still is to waste time; the goal of life is to have; whatever (or whoever) is old is obsolete; permanent commitment is impossible and undesirable; being radical means denying what went before. And then he concluded that mortification arises from a different way of seeing the world: "It is the one activity that resists the enchantment of affluence, that raises questions about the bewitching promises of pleasure that the great Western mirage machine turns out

---

1. James Carroll, "Mortification for Liberation," *National Catholic Reporter,* December 10, 1971.

in an infinity of packages. Mortification arises from the gut instinct that the Buick is *not* something to believe in."

I would like to suggest that the psychology and asceticism of celibacy lie in the fact that it too is an act of radical doubt about a number of things that our culture takes for granted. I am not saying that this is the only function or meaning of religious celibacy, nor am I saying that this is the most useful way to view it. But I do think it may open up some avenues for personal growth and for speaking some provocative word to the contemporary world.

I would like to single out four issues or questions that modern man is struggling with: (1) How is sexuality related to the development of full humanness? (2) How can I overcome loneliness? (3) What is masculinity-femininity? (4) How can I achieve self-fulfillment?

SEXUALITY AND FULL HUMANNESS

The first issue arises out of the present-day cultural assumption that direct sexual experience is necessary for full human development. Because sex is as natural to us as eating, the argument goes, we will become stunted in our growth as persons unless we have a regular, guilt-free experience of sexual ecstasy. So strongly has this assumption taken root in our society that psychiatrists on college campuses have pointed out a curious phenomenon: formerly students would complain of tension and guilt over their sexual experiences; nowadays they suffer tension and guilt about still being virgins! This is what Eugene Kennedy has called "sexual fascism,"[2] the notion that full human-

---

2. Eugene Kennedy, *The New Sexuality: Myths, Fables, and Hang-Ups* (Garden City: Doubleday, 1972), Chapter 2.

ness is impossible without gratification of the sex drive. James Carroll sees it as a chauvinist idea, particularly when applied to the male: "To say, as American culture does, that sexual abstinence makes a full life impossible for a man, that every man needs a bed-fellow, is to endorse and continue the idea that the woman exists primarily to satisfy the man's needs, to console him, to support him while he does the world's serious work."[3]

To choose celibacy, then, is an act of radical doubt about the link between sexual experience and development of humanness. It is to challenge the cultural idols of hedonism and consumerism. It is to assert that a person, man or woman, can become fully human within the context of sexual abstinence. The attractive personality of Jesus is the concrete witness that one can be both truly human and celibate. The witness is diluted, of course, every time the world encounters a cold, frightened, or insensitive celibate whose growth is stunted. Yet psychological research shows that the incidence of sexual difficulties and immaturities is no greater or less among celibates than among non-celibates. Psychologist Abraham Maslow points out that it is not abstinence as such that is pathogenic, but the feelings or motivations accompanying it:

> It is now well known that many cases are found in which celibacy has no psychopathological effects. In other cases, however, it has many bad effects. What factor determines which shall be the result? Clinical work with non-neurotic people gives the clear answer that sexual deprivation becomes pathogenic in the severe sense only when it is felt by the individual to represent rejection by the opposite sex, inferiority, lack of worth, lack of re-

---

3. Carroll, "Mortification for Liberation."

spect, isolation, or other thwarting of basic needs. Sexual deprivation can be borne with relative ease by individuals for whom it has no such implication.[4]

THE ISSUE OF LONELINESS

The second issue is that of loneliness. The existentialists have focused attention on the human condition of separateness and man's need to overcome the distance between himself and others. "It is not good for man to be alone" (Gen 2:18). It is crucial for mental health to know that we are prized, valued, cared about—and to know that someone else needs us. Moreover, sociologists have shown that the mass society in which we live serves to reinforce our sense of isolation. As Howard and Charlotte Clinebell put it:

> Many factors in our society militate against depth relationships: the frenzied pace of our lives; the frantic pressures to get ahead which encourage using rather than relating to people; the constant mobility of many families which contributes to rootlessness and non-involvement in community life; the anonymity of megalopolis where people do not know the names of even those in adjoining apartments. . . . From his long experience in working with emotionally disturbed children, Bruno Bettleheim declares, "The more we live in a mass society, the more important are intimate relationships."[5]

---

4. Abraham Maslow, *Motivation and Personality* (New York: Harper and Row, 1954); quoted in Frank Goble, *The Third Force* (New York: Pocket Books, 1971), p. 78.

5. Howard and Charlotte Clinebell, *The Intimate Marriage* (New York: Harper and Row, 1970), p. 18.

The Clinebells and others[6] believe that this need for intimacy is the primary, if not only, motivation for marriage today, since every other function of marriage and family can be fulfilled in some other way. And here is where the celibate throws in another radical doubt: maybe marriage is not the only way to overcome our loneliness. In his little book *The Art of Loving,* Erich Fromm says that our sense of isolation can be transcended in many ways: by friendship, by fraternal groups, by the service of others, by the love of God. He has some other very healthy things to say about love. He points out that much of the misunderstanding about love in our culture is that too much emphasis is placed on the *object* of love rather than on the function of loving. That is, people think that to love is easy—it comes naturally; the big problem is to find the right "object" or person to love. Often those who have never loved anyone are convinced that they will immediately learn to love as soon as the right person comes along. Fromm rejects this as a naive fallacy. He insists that love is an art; it must be learned and developed and purified in a lifelong struggle against the tendency to regress into selfishness. Love cannot terminate in one person alone, to the exclusion of all others. If it does, it most probably is not love at all, but mutual egoism. The most important thing in life is that we become loving persons, that we deepen our capacity to love and be loved.[7]

And this is precisely the vision of the celibate. He or she feels the same need to love and be loved as anyone else. The Greeley and Kennedy studies on the priesthood

---

6. See, for example, Gail P. Fullerton, *Survival in Marriage* (New York: Holt, Rinehart and Winston, 1972), especially Chapter 2.

7. Erich Fromm, *The Art of Loving* (New York: Harper and Row, 1956), pp. 1–4.

have shown that loneliness is one of the major problems in the lives of American priests. My own experience in counseling is that the same is true of religious, both men and women. At the same time, my experience in marriage counseling has taught me that the incidence of loneliness and unfulfilled needs for affection is as high among the married as it is among celibates, and that marriage is no guarantee of growth in the capacity to love. The witness that the celibate priest or religious can offer the world is that to become a loving, giving person is much more humanizing than the frantic search for intimacy and recognition.

Moreover, the deeper asceticism of celibacy is that loneliness and the need for intimacy can be transcended. At times, at least, we celibates must learn to stand alone. Our vocation calls us to give more than to receive. People will not always appreciate our work; they will often take us for granted; sometimes the "hard sayings" we proclaim will alienate. One of my priest-clients who was hurting from these experiences in ministry tried to justify a "Third Way" relationship with a woman by saying: "Many priests I know wrap themselves around a bottle instead of a woman." The question is, of course, why must it be the one or the other? Why not stand free and give ourselves in love to those in need? To quote James Carroll again:

> The celibate life is a tough and slightly unnatural way to live. It requires a knowledge of mortification that is as concrete as an empty bed each morning. But it makes sense and gives its own kind of satisfaction when the needs of the served community and the presence of God and the priest's own freedom are all more important than his loneliness.[8]

---

8. Carroll, "Mortification for Liberation."

MASCULINITY-FEMININITY

The third cultural issue that is addressed by the asceticism of celibacy is the whole question of masculinity-femininity. American males, in particular, are terribly self-conscious about this. "Are you really a man?" is the stabbing question the male feels every time he sees a TV commercial starring Joe Namath. And, sooner or later, "being a man" comes to be translated in terms of sexual performance. For centuries of human history, a man's virility was demonstrated by the number of children he could produce. And even in today's contraceptive society, sterility is still a cause of anxiety. But the real "proof" of masculinity nowadays is the ability of the man to bring his woman to orgasm. Underlying this is another chauvinist assumption: that most women are depressed and miserable about their sex lives and that they are longing for some male savior to liberate them. This is the fantasy that Eugene Kennedy has labeled "the great orgasm hunt."[9] And Rollo May calls it "the tyranny of the orgasm," because its effect is often just the opposite: because both man and woman are so anxious to achieve total and simultaneous orgasm, their very tension makes it impossible.[10]

Again, a celibate life style calls into radical doubt these inadequate images of masculinity-femininity. It is true that for many celibates not having children of their own is one of the deepest renunciations of celibacy. At the same time, this choice of life points to something more profound than either orgasm or offspring as a sign of potency. I believe Erik Erikson has captured it in his beauti-

---

9. Kennedy, *New Sexuality,* Chapter 4.

10. Rollo May, *Love and Will* (New York: Norton, 1969), pp. 44, 53–57.

ful concept of "generativity," which he defines as "the concern for establishing and guiding the next generation."[11] This is what gives an adult man or woman a sense of vitality, of making some contribution to the world, of leaving behind oneself something positive and permanent. Erikson sees this need being fulfilled directly in parenthood; but he also has an opening for "sublimated parenthood" in which persons may choose to direct their caring to others than their own children. The important thing is that the adult have a sense of generativity—that he is building, creating, participating in life and doing something valuable.

The celibate believes that he or she will attain a sense of generativity through creative work and through loving relationships with people. To the question: "Who is truly a man or a woman?" the celibate answers: *one who gives life to others.* This is why Erich Fromm says: "Love is a power which produces love; impotence is the inability to produce love."[12] So it is the life-giving quality of love that makes for true generativity. Depending on how we live it, our celibacy can render us either sterile or productive. We are called to give of that which is most alive in us: the riches of the total Christian mystery; the faith, hope, and love that animate us; the deep sense of union with Christ that drives us on. In Fromm's analysis of love, there is no place for sacrifice as such; giving of oneself is supposed to be intrinsically rewarding, not painful, because it enhances one's sense of being alive. But we celibates know that the constant effort to love others chastely and unselfishly is often painful. Our joy in self-giving springs not only from a

---

11. Erik Erikson, *Identity: Youth and Crisis* (New York: Norton, 1968), p. 138.

12. Fromm, *The Art of Loving,* p. 25.

sense of being alive, but even more from the conviction that we are striving to give life, and that this can only happen, according to the Gospel, if we are willing to die to our self, like the grain of wheat.

LIFE AS SELF-FULFILLMENT

And that leads into the fourth area where the asceticism of celibacy confronts one of the assumptions of modern man—the assumption, namely, that the purpose of life is self-fulfillment. I remember vividly my last year in the seminary in 1959. One of our professors was giving us an inspired ferverino on how we ought to see ourselves in relationship to the Church. "You should find your greatest joy," he said, "in giving yourselves completely to the service of the Church. You should desire no life of your own. You should let yourself be used by the Church in whatever way it needs you. Whatever job you're given, you should see it as filling a hole until somebody better comes along."

I suppose it is amazing enough that he should say such things and really be convinced of them. But what is even more amazing is that we accepted them. That was the spirituality of self-sacrifice, of being consumed by a cause greater than yourself. And it appealed to our idealism.

But a lot has happened in fifteen years. If the upheavals of the 1960's have accomplished nothing else, they have certainly unmasked the self-serving ideologies hidden behind this kind of rhetoric. We see more clearly now that the language and spirituality of self-sacrifice can be used to legitimate abuses of power by those in authority. "Be obedient to your superiors" can be translated: "Do as you're told and don't ask questions." "Be a good servant of the Church" often meant "Don't threaten our position as masters." As one ideology after another was found wanting, as one institution after another lost credibility, people no longer found anything outside themselves in which they could invest their psychic energy. The vacuum was filled by the ideology of self-fulfillment: what is most important is that I develop as a person, that I actualize all my potentialities. Our consciousness was raised. It was degrading, we were told, to allow ourselves to be used by any bureaucracy or institution. It was oppressive to be robbed of our right to self-determination, creativity, and the pursuit of personal goals. In this kind of philosophical milieu, it is no wonder that the celibate found himself in a painful position. There he stood, feeling he had been seduced into celibacy without being fully aware of it, and deprived of the opportunity to develop the kind of intimate relationship that offered so much promise of personal fulfillment.

For the truth is, celibacy does cast a radical doubt upon the whole philosophy of self-fulfillment. The celibate dares to question whether there is something deeper or more transcendent in man than the drive to actualize himself. Viktor Frankl put it very well when he said that self-fulfillment is like happiness: if sought for its own sake, it eludes us. It must be seen as a by-product, a consequence, of something else—what Frankl calls "meaning" or "self-transcendence." Man will fulfill himself, he says, only insofar as he finds meaning in, and commits himself to, something or someone outside of himself.[13]

Here it is useful to recall that the Church has always taught that celibacy itself is of no value for its own sake. It

---

13. Viktor Frankl, *The Will to Meaning* (New York: World, 1960), pp. 38ff.

is only celibacy "for the sake of the kingdom" that is recognized as a Christian evangelical counsel. The man who chooses celibacy is presumed to have had *an experience of the love of God.* This experience captivates him, it lights up and relativizes all other values. It gives rise to the desire to "build the kingdom"—to witness to the grace-filled presence of God in the midst of the human, to communicate the redemptive love of God to all peoples.

The most powerful witness value of celibacy, it seems to me, is not eschatological but incarnational. Certainly, the celibate points to a fulfillment yet to come. But even more directly, he or she points to a present reality: God is here, and he cares. This is symbolized by the caring of the celibate, a caring that transcends family ties and embraces all who are in need. Our celibate vocation calls us to a radical kind of loving. It calls us to love as Christ loved—universally and non-selectively: not just the bright, young, and appreciative, but also the crank, the dependent, the neurotic, the ungrateful. What I am suggesting is that a celibate lifestyle is a way of witnessing to the Christian belief that man is called beyond self-fulfillment to self-transcendence. It is by forgetting himself that a man will truly actualize himself.

THE AFFIRMATIONS OF CELIBACY

We have seen, then, that the choice of celibacy is an act of radical doubt about four assumptions deeply rooted in our culture. But I would prefer to state it more positively: the choice of celibacy reflects a series of affirmations about the quality of human life. Celibacy is indeed an act of renunciation. But every renunciation is also an affirmation: I renounce that because I value this more highly. The

Latin word "renuntiare" means "to proclaim again"; it is an act of affirmation, free of the negative connotations we usually give to the word "renounce." When I choose celibacy, I am not negating any human good or value; I am relativizing some values in order to give a more central place to others. In particular, I am proclaiming: (1) that the development of full humanness is more important than sexual expression; (2) that becoming a loving person is more important than overcoming loneliness; (3) that true generativity is greater than sexual potency; (4) that self-transcendence is more fully human than self-fulfillment.

THE GRUMPY CHILDREN OF GOD

But none of these values will be authentically affirmed unless celibates themselves are warm, vital, loving persons. In my experience, the most frequent syndrome I have found among priests and religious is what I would call a "low-key hostility." These are not angry people; they are quietly and passively resentful. They resent the burdens of celibacy, the ineptness of religious leadership, the confusion of theology, and the ingratitude of the faithful. Their prayer life—or lack of it—will often reveal that the low-key hostility is also directed at God; somehow he has let them down. Henri Nouwen calls these people "the grumpy children of God."[14]

My own belief is that the problem goes much deeper than the issue of celibacy. I believe the roots of the problem are sociological and cultural. Religious men and wom-

---

14. Henri Nouwen, "From Resentment to Gratitude" (unpublished lecture).

en have experienced a stunning loss of status, a painful deglamorization of the religious life. As a result, a good number of religious are no longer proud of their profession. They have the terrible feeling of being outsiders; they so much want to give, but nobody seems to need them. This is that painful experience of "non-validation" spoken about in the document on the spiritual renewal of the American priesthood: "It is a cruel suffering to feel useless, out of date, not needed, rejected; to experience the conflict of having to preach a Gospel the people do not want to hear."[15]

ACCEPTING OUR PURIFIED STATUS

So it seems to me that this is the context in which we need to develop an asceticism of celibacy. I have no complete program, but I believe it must include at least several elements. For one thing, we need to accept our purified status. The people of prestige today are the research scientists, the educators, the journalists, the news analysts. But nowhere in the New Testament does Jesus ever promise prestige. In fact, every time the subject of status came up among the apostles, he rebuked them for quarreling about it. What he did offer was a ministry of service. The simple fact is that we are broken people trying to mend a broken world. We religious can become melodramatic about the agonies of our lives; we can let ourselves revel in self-pity or what Nouwen calls "spiritual exhibitionism."[16] What we need is the ability to stand with dignity in our purified

15. E. Larkin and G. Broccolo, *Spiritual Renewal of the American Priesthood* (Washington: NCCB, 1972), p. 20.

16. Henri Nouwen, *The Wounded Healer* (Garden City: Doubleday, 1972), p. 60.

status, to reach out and comfort others even when we are hurting ourselves. If we are humble enough, compassionate enough, and gutsy enough to risk, we will find ourselves at the center of people's lives, not standing around at the periphery.

PURITY OF HEART

This is why the celibate's love needs to be disciplined by purity of heart. I am not using "purity" here in the sense of chastity, but in Kierkegaard's sense of "Purity of heart is to will only one thing." The "one thing" in this case is the growth of the other person or persons. Research in psychotherapy has demonstrated that true growth and healing take place only in a relationship characterized by love. The ever-present danger is that the therapist will use the relationship with the client to gratify his own needs. When this happens, therapy is inevitably a failure. The therapist helps only when he loves the client unselfishly and non-possessively. It is the same way in religious life. It is so easy to use people to further our own self-interest—to get them to admire us, depend on us, have them all to ourselves, and so on. It is only purity of heart that will enable us to love others warmly and genuinely, yet allow them to be free.

Charles Curran, the priest-psychologist, uses an interesting image to bring out this element of detachment in celibate love.[17] He points to the mythical image of the hero, and its cultural translation, the American cowboy. He reminds us that the cowboy in folklore is usually in

---

17. Charles A. Curran, *Psychological Dynamics in Religious Living* (New York: Herder and Herder, 1981).

some way a redemptive figure. He enters the "unre-deemed" town, identifies with the people, and delivers them from evil by his own goodness. Sometimes he ends up marrying the town beauty; but more often than not, he rides off alone to continue his work somewhere else. If he does form a close relationship with a woman, it is a non-possessive relationship. In the novel *Shane,* for example, the cowboy becomes close friends with a husband and wife and their young son. At the showdown, when he has to fight the gunslinger, the wife tries to talk him out of risking his life. He answers: "Look, I'm not doing this just for you; I'm doing it for all three of you." Curran's con-clusion is that the celibate's vocation is to love in such a way as to bind other people together, not come between them. The celibate is an instrument of reconciliation, and for that he or she needs purity of heart.

THE NEED FOR SUPPORT

The other side of the coin, though (and this would be a third element in the asceticism of celibacy), is that reli-gious do need support systems. They are not mythical he-roes, they are flesh-and-blood human beings. The document on the spiritual renewal of the American priest-hood puts a great deal of stress on this:

The American priest needs others—his bishop, his brother priests, and those with whom he shares a deep faith—to provide personal interest and perhaps actual presence in his prayer life. Left alone, he can too easily crawl into the hole his guilts have dug for him. Left alone, he can easily divorce his prayer life from his min-isterial activity. Left alone, he does not have the usual instrument the Lord uses to sharpen and purify faith, namely, a community of faith.

The document here is talking about prayer, but I think the point of support extends to all areas of our life. One of the healthiest things I see developing today is the formation of small groups of priests and religious, not just to enjoy bowling or golf together, but to share their faith, their work, their ideals, and their struggles. Priests and religious are learning the value of real friendships.

THE ATTITUDE OF LOOKING BEYOND

There is one other element I would like to single out for an asceticism of celibacy, and that is the attitude of "looking beyond." This is that "contemplative vision of reality" that James Carroll talks about. Our American mentality has conditioned us to think in terms of efficiency, productivity, growth curves, and the like. It is easy for us to carry over this mentality into the work of the ministry. And in some sense I think we should. That is why I am helping my Order develop a system of accountability. It is important for people to know that they are investing their energies wisely and have something to show for their work. At the same time, there is a great deal of ambiguity here. How do you measure "success" in ministry? How do you assess "impact"? When we turn to the Scriptures, we find that they are never impressed by numbers or by power—only that faith is being proclaimed in word and in action, that witness is being given. It is clear that man's efforts alone cannot make the Kingdom happen; he must wait for the Lord. For myself, I have stopped hoping for a "great spiritual renewal" in my time. I do not think it will happen. I am content to be an "interim man"—standing firm in a time of upheaval, trying to build bridges between the Church of the past and the Church of the future. At the same time, the attitude of "looking beyond" also means seeing God's activity in the here-and-now, even though it seems small in scale. I see it, for example, in the struggles of my counselees trying to become their better self. I see it in the many priests and religious I know who are giving great service to the people of God. I see it in what I think will be the long-range good effects of the present structural and attitudinal changes in liturgy, in religious education, and in Church authority.

CONCLUSION

In this article I have not tried to examine, much less resolve, all the tensions inherent in religious celibacy. My purpose has been twofold. First, I have proposed that one way to see celibacy as a meaningful life style is to view it as an act of radical doubt about some values in the culture that easily become idolatrous, and as an act of affirmation about some human and Gospel values that easily get submerged in the culture. Second, I have suggested that the low-key hostility and resentment that celibates often display is related to the wider context of the crisis in Church ministry and that this calls for an asceticism or spirituality not only of celibacy but of religious life itself. For me, what unites all these threads is the theme of the paschal mystery. It seems to me that celibacy, mortification, purity of heart, service, contemplative vision—all are forms of dying to self and rising to new life in Christ, so that I can be more life-giving, more generative, more loving toward the people I serve.

Two Ways of Loving

VIRGINIA SULLIVAN FINN

WHEN I WAS A VERY LITTLE GIRL, I thought story-telling was the ordinary, everyday way of communication for many people because my father always talked by telling stories. His favorite Church story was about his own pastor, the one who tried to baptize him Bartholomew Cornelius, the pastor's name, instead of Thomas Edward, the name my grandparents had chosen.

It seems that the pastor stopped suddenly, mid-sentence, early in his sermon, one summer Sunday, to stalk down the aisle and out of the church. Grabbing a whip from a carriage, the pastor proceeded to beat a horse gone wild in the street. When the task was accomplished, he resumed his place in the pulpit to finish his sermon with only a single reference to the incident. "Any unruly horse, woman, or passion, you must whip into submission!"

It's good at times to remember our past—and to remind ourselves that the Church has changed, somewhat, since that day. John and Mary* are caught up in those

---

*John and Mary are religious who in their late twenties fall in love.

changes and in the uncertain currents of our time. Rather than center on the specificities of their present situation, however, I will try to unfold dynamics pertaining to relationships between men and women, particularly priests and women.

In discussing this, my hope is that what follows will be a dialogue with you, that you will test what is said in relation to your own experience, hopes, aims, and spirituality.

Evaluating distinctions between coupling and intentional friendship will be the focus of this paper. Coupling will refer to a relationship between two persons who share both emotional affectivity and, partially or completely, a sexually active relationship. Intentional friendship will refer to a relationship between two persons who feel emotional affectivity for one another without sharing partial or complete sexual activity. Both forms of relationship imply that the two persons, in addition to knowing one another in other encounters, spend time alone together, regularly or sporadically. In both forms of relationship the two may be seen together alone in public, having lunch or attending a lecture together, for example. In other words, the distinctions considered significant between the two forms of relationship are not external.

Because of its length in years and its demand for total mutual sharing and responsibility, only the marriage relationship can fruitfully encompass both coupling and friendship. Marriage is also often more than marriage. When it is family, children force both growth and stability in the couple and provide an opportunity for spouses to combine coupling and friendship. Marriage, of course, can have its terrors and times when neither coupling nor friendship characterizes it.

A few notes pertaining only to intentional friendship are in order before we make comparisons. In this type of relationship the man may yearn sexually for the woman; she may desire him the same way. But both man and woman already have other primary commitments (such as marriage, religious life, or priesthood). Because of this, it is necessary to keep in mind that these persons are part of a socialization pattern that includes many other relationships besides the one described.

Our dialogue will center on two questions. Like many of us, John and Mary must face these questions. The first pertains to unity: What does "the two of us together" mean in our relationship? The second relates to affectivity: How do we deal with the strong emotional feelings that may emerge between the two of us?

THE UNITY OF COUPLING

Let us speak first, then, of unity. Our images of unity are formed by our pasts, and the dynamic of bonding in creatures has hidden roots. Scientists are helping us unearth some of these roots and their effects:

We have all seen ducklings following their mother in a line. Experimenters have discovered that it is necessary for the duckling to hear its mother make the quacking sound when the duckling is between thirteen and sixteen hours old. [This] makes a unique and permanent impression on the brain. . . . If the duckling hears the quack at the critical hour, but the mother is not in sight, the duckling will imprint on whatever is in sight. It might be a farmer or even a dog. And it will follow that person or animal thereafter.

In our formative years these kinds of bondings become intertwined with images of power, possession, and
responsibility. Children, in a sense, own their parents
through their demand that the feelings, spirit, intellect,
and bodies of parents be used in care for them. Parents,
because of the power of their position, have command
over their children, their intellect, spirit, bodies, and in
the creation of their feelings.

This may account for why the bonding sense rever-
berates with such strength in cultures and cannot be avoided. Images of a father lifting his daughter high on his
shoulders and of a mother nursing her baby son, as much
as overt sexual images, tell us that flesh touching flesh is
intimate, endearing, and one.

We bring this "sense" with us to adulthood and experience it as adults in the cultural mores around us. That
may be why oneness is implied in sexual sharing. There is,
in flesh, a giving over and a taking, an entry into another
and a leaving of self. In the coupling, because of the depth
of the physicality and the affectivity, each person may experience a new freedom through this unity, but each also,
in a sense, abandons freedom to the elusive spirit of owning that emerges in sexual oneness. Owned by you I realize I owe to you.

By free choice, I have, through coupling, become
part of a dynamic that now limits my choice unless hedonism is my style. This judgment is not an invention of the
magisterium or theologians. It emerges from the mono-
gram of passion, the mutual intertwining into one of two
emotions, two spirits, and two bodies. This is a phenome-
nological truth in all persons who cherish wholeness in human beings. This is a truth John and Mary must face.

Within, yet also beyond, the affection that we have
for one another, I discover that your flesh calls me back to

you; you discover my flesh calls you back to me. Through the particularities and certainties of touch we remember one another. You may remember me in my specificity, but if we are coupled we also share a unified memory of oneness, a "two-of-us-together-touching-through-flesh-in-space-and-time" memory. This memory enables and encourages us to fantasize from known experience, not guessed hope. We are urged by it to anticipate with a sureness that heightens the desire.

My desire for you lures me into surrendering to the small coercions you demand of me for our unity. You also willingly compromise because you, too, cherish our oneness. Because who each of us is is tied to who we are together and we have symbolized this with our bodies, our unity is our oneness. This glory we cherish and protect.

The two of us together, in the coupling form of relationship, inevitably means exclusivity. There is at least one dimension between us, our shared sexual pleasure, that others cannot opt into without specific invitation which we will not give. Unless one is part of a milieu with an immature or coarse set of values, flesh is inevitably a closed bonding, one that has an owning and owing sense.

THE UNITY OF FRIENDSHIP

In the face of all this what can be said for simple friendship? Although this is a question a man and woman with other primary commitments, like John and Mary, may ask themselves, it is a question our general culture seems to leave unanswered. Only in the experience itself will we discover what the unity of intentional friendship is.

The two of us in intentional friendship means inclusivity—open bonding, relinquishing possession. There is no one dimension we share together that you may not share with another. That is my gift to you in our friendship. Although confidences we share will not be shared with others, any dimension of myself that I share with you, I may also share with others. That is your gift to me in our friendship.

In our intentional friendship, complementarity is the dynamic of our unity. Because we have forsaken the freedom to establish our oneness in flesh, we are free to look deeply into each other as the separate persons we are. I discover realities about you I did not know, and you may not have known yourself. I am, in turn, being explored and discovered in the same way. When exploring you, I surrender myself in attending to you, and you do the same with me. A fresh experience of self emerges along with a fresh experience of you. Because of this, true friends such as we never tire of one another.

Though the man and woman may crave at times for physical bonding, they need no physical bond or outward revelation of affectivity for unity. In intentional friendship each tests the other in truth. This renews trust which is the bond.

I am myself with you. You are yourself with me. We have no memories held by the sharing of the particularities and certainties of sensual touching. Our unity dwells in the more elusive realm of sensing. And this is risk. I cannot be sure that what I sense is what you feel. Without the flesh to call each of us back to the other, our fidelity to one another rests entirely on trust. There is no ownership. There is, however, the owing that my faith in you, and your faith in me, invites.

Because sexual activity is uninvited, no place can be

set for it at table. We must talk about the specificity you are, or about the specificity I am, or about cabbages and kings, but never affectionately about us in oneness.

If trust wears thin or if intentionality goes slack, our friendship can easily die, not by burning up but by the atrophy of talk that has forgotten who the two of us can be together. "Didn't we know each other better two years ago a little past eight in the evening . . . in September I think it was?"

You cannot take me in your arms to heal the hurt you've sent my way. I cannot tell you "I didn't mean what I said" by soothing your body with my hands. Between us lies a trust that will never be celebrated by enfleshed symbol, yet this trust is the glory our unity gifts us with. Because it is our only bond, this fragile trust must be protected as we would protect our physical oneness were we coupled.

In intentional friendship the two-of-us-together does not mean oneness. Each of us, more completely "himself" and "herself," does not make the "changes for his sake" and "conversions for her sake," without which oneness would never come into being. The harmony of the relationship is determined by man and woman appreciating the uniqueness of each other while navigating the shoals created by "her impossible side" and "his stubbornness." Though he may steady her when life for her is an earthquake, he'll do it his way, and not in a way that has emerged from their oneness. Being herself, she may switch from gentle sympathy to playful teasing in the twinkling of an eye.

Having looked at the dynamic of unity in each relationship, it is time to study the differences in emotional dynamics between coupling and intentional friendship.

EMOTIONAL DYNAMICS IN COUPLING

In coupling, merger through sexual pleasure and openly expressed affectivity makes you part of me. I love you, but I especially love the you in "us." Each of us shares a physical and affective center, openly experienced and remembered by both of us. We are caught up in its aura. This enchantment and pleasure binds us, at least temporarily, and together we plan for the next time when we can share the same feelings and activity. We yearn for that sameness and suffer disappointment if it is thwarted.

At the same time, our sexual sharing in coupling and the affectivity that accompanies it builds a "sheltering us" that becomes a home to absorb all the problems each of us has. Because we have opened the door to taking responsibility for fulfilling each other's sexual needs, expectations in relation to other responsibilities increase through our deepened sense of oneness. This may be why persons who could without difficulty share sexually while living apart drift toward living together. Sexual sharing easily becomes a magnet for "telling all"—and giving all even though the man or woman may sense that this is not the one with whom "I want to tell all" or give all.

Holding back can become a grave issue in coupling. If in the coupling relationship between two persons with other primary commitments partial sexual activity takes place, there may be a physical holding back to insure that passion does not lead to completion. If completion is the style of the relationship, there may likewise be subtle gestures, looks, remarks, or outright arguments that caution the other to remember that "I am not owned by you." This lie, if converted into truth, might tip the tower of jackstraws toward desertion of one's primary commitment. The degree of control and the drain on energy sexual coupling demands of persons with other primary commitments subverts the freedom the couple felt initially. Without an affective focus on "us," the sexual activity loses emotional valuation and may become only recreational (mutual masturbation). With an affective focus on "us," emotions make it difficult to keep the relationship in a fixed, cautionary position; it insists on moving, growing, changing, deepening, exploding in a frenzy of love or hate.

When they happen, and later when we remember, we savor those moments of tenderness, of gentle humor and magnificent passion, and of hurts healed. Yet we know that affectivity and sexual activity, united, are by themselves unaware of the rest of the world. They make unseasonable demands because the heart and the body never reason. "But I need you tonight! I don't want to be alone!" "What do you mean something came up? We planned to be together today!"

EMOTIONAL DYNAMICS OF FRIENDSHIP

On first reading, intentional friendship between two persons with other primary commitments appears to be no better a state. Because the emotional focus that might provide the entrance for sexual activity must by effort not be allowed to emerge, friendship appears, at first glance, less free. Unity based on complementarity means that we invite one another not to center on "us in oneness." This does not mean that "us" is not talked about. In intentional friendship it is crucial to share occasionally how each of us feels about the "us" that we are. That "us," however, is not the "us of oneness." We would be deceptive if we did not talk frankly without the affectionate endearments that would lend a romantic aura to our language, mood, and need. The style and words of our dialogue acknowledge that the depth of our feeling for one another is a problem as well as a joy. We do not push the world away in order to speak of love as couples do.

Your focus is on me, not us, and mine is on you, not us. My feelings are free to plummet to the deepest levels of compassion for you, of appreciation and gratitude for you, of anger when you do not realize your gifts or you cut short honesty about yourself to me. From you I receive the same depth. We know how to argue. We know how to give. Most of all, while together, we know how to resist affectivity that would pull us into what we may both desire but have committed ourselves not to have. We have posited "oneness" elsewhere, in our primary commitments, and are free, with the above exception, to be an unencumbered "me and you" together.

In our relationship of friendship, moreover, because it is not coupling, we do not "plan" that we will share the same emotions at the same time, a pattern necessary in sexual affairs. I want you to come to me just as you are. You want the same from me. We are open to this other risk and to coincidence. The joy that comes is always spontaneous, and thus an epiphany.

Complementarity rather than oneness means that, by holding back an active physicality and the affectivity that leads to physicality, I am free to feel more deeply for you as you are, and you for me as I am, because we perceive phenomenologically our separateness. As noted earlier, merger through sexual pleasure and openly expressed affectivity makes you part of me, drawing love from me for the you in "us." In intentional friendship, on the other hand, I love the you in you, and let you love the me in me without insisting that that me unite with that you. This is a loss that can, in time, become a found.

Say I am celibate, you are married. My oneness is commitment to God through community and Church. Your oneness is commitment to God through marriage and Church. My celibacy is part of who I am; my community is part of who I am. That wholeness of me you have come to love. You respect my celibate dimension as much as my other dimensions. I would not be me without it. If, for a time, I become estranged from oneness with my community or the Church, what is your role as friend? If you were a counselor, you might isolate the estrangement in order to help me express and resolve all the negative and positive feelings I have in regard to it. If you assumed the role of a superior or a pastor, you might remind me of the ethical dimension of myself and challenge my loyalty to promises I had made.

But you are my friend. You love me in my wholeness. Instead of isolating a part of me, you help me remember who I have been in the past and who I had hoped to be in the future in that wholeness. You help me struggle with who I am in the present, suffering with me as I reflect on the source of that estrangement, affirming me as I try to resolve that estrangement. As I lose my sense of my wholeness, you, as friend, do not.

If you take this estrangement and suffering as opportunity to offer me oneness elsewhere—that is, with you— you are, suddenly and most regrettably, no longer my friend. The love you offer is a love that has forgotten who I am.

When a person's primary commitment becomes vulnerable because of the situation in which it is, for moment, being lived, the fascination of coupling can become intense. Surrendering to this fascination may overwhelm fidelity to primary commitment; then the person is thrust into comparing a "honeymoon" type of oneness with a "honeymoon-is-over" type of oneness. For the long-term relationship that one has within religious community or marriage is inevitably a "honeymoon-is-over" kind of oneness. There may be greater depth and deeper joys, but these are seldom isolated from the strife and challenge and frustration that is realistic everyday life.

Coupling, that phenomenon many men and women as well as the media cling to in enthusiasm for romantic escape, serves as a cushion against the "upheaval reality" we encounter in a free society day after day. The popularity of coupling should not surprise us, for coupling, at first, promises and delivers release from "upheaval reality" because coupling, with its honeymoon spirit, is always isolation. In coupling you and I find a cocoon. Because it diverts us from dealing with reality it may disengage us from deeper emotions. Eventually, ennui may pervade our relationship. "What went wrong?" we ask ourselves.

Coupling, as a life style, is linked with the demise of the spirit of qualitative generativity—caring beyond self for others in the civic-communal, more universal, sense. The malaise concerning motivation in regard to celibacy should not be seen apart from this.

Young celibates and candidates for celibacy were raised in today's culture. To isolate issues concerning them from attitudes of their counterparts in the secular culture is unwise. On the other hand, commentators who shout "Halleluia!" in celebration of coupling, and critics who shout "Sin!" in a burst of condemnation and dismissal, are on the same side, for both the acclaimers and the detractors turn their backs on the imperative task, the serious search for roots and resolutions.

Couplings, homosexual unions, living together, single parenting, and some divorces share a similarity with the race to suburbia of recent years. They provide an escape from the mobility and upheaval reality of our culture. At times, segregation of priests from people or rigid sex segregation in relationships between men and women in the Church or even community itself can be used as an escape from contemporary reality. That all these escape phenomena are now contributing to the alienation that creates upheaval reality would be ironic if it were not tragic. Strict codes of behavior, old rhetoric, new rhetoric are hollow solutions. Instead, men and women committed to facing upheaval reality and to relating with affective fidelity to one another and to their vows may help the Church become the generative witness of Christ it is called to be.

In this paper I have attempted a "seeing more deeply into what is before our eyes." Because the commentary on friendship has been limited to one set of two persons in relationship does not mean that only one intentional friendship in a person's life is being suggested. Pseudo-marriage is not recommended. A vowed person is more likely to remain a vowed person if he or she has several intentional friendships with persons of the opposite sex.

An analogy might help in summing up this "seeing what is before our eyes." Suppose you are in a museum. You enter a room with a large, many-sided stone, exhibited on a stand. Each side of the stone represents a different life style within a life span of a contemporary person in our culture. Six sides represent variations in the style of marriage. Marriage: without children; with children; with divorce followed by marriage; preceded by living together; preceded and followed by couplings or combined with couplings; combined with family and intentional friendships. Three sides represent the single state: with sexual couplings; as live-together relationships; as limited to intentional friendships. Religious life and priesthood are represented by three sides: without couplings or intentional friendships; with couplings; with intentional friendships.

The variety available surprises you. You look more closely and run your hand over each side. Your hand is scratched by the roughness and scraped as it slips into the clefts and crevices within the stone.

"One smooth and perfect side cannot be found," you murmur. If I were with you I would agree. There is no escape from upheaval reality. It is inherent in each life style, each life span. There is no side without night and cross. We are naive at this time to succumb to the new coupling rhetoric of our age or the old segregation rhetoric of another age.

Solidarity is the dynamic some men and women are already beginning to live. Relationships of friendship, they are discovering, can enhance one's identity as person, increase one's compassion, give one a renewed sense of being and strength, and enrich the Catholic community, helping it to be generative toward the wholeness that family, community, Church, and culture can be.

We have reflected on coupling and intentional friendship. They are an either . . . or. There are two distinctly different dynamics to the two forms of knowing. Each has its own specific, fulfilling dynamic that cannot be avoided.

John, in our case study, might not feel ready to embark on the kind of friendship described here were his relationship with Mary to end, and in that decision he would be wise. His openness with his spiritual director may help him avoid, however, merely drifting into a life style by isolating this or that dimension of himself without regard to the wholeness of himself as a human being, a temptation some of his brothers and his counterparts in the culture might give way to.

How John has been educated within the society in regard to sexuality and relationships is beyond the spiritual director's domain but not beyond relevancy to the case. If he has received a multiplicity of conflicting directives—be affective here, don't be affective there; be affective this way but not that—without rhyme, reason, or clarity, paralysis can easily set in.

Perhaps John has not seen, in the generation that models the priesthood for him, examples of fruitful relationships with the opposite sex; if so, it is no wonder that marriage comes to mind as the one and only alternative available if one does not wish to be isolated from affectivity in relation to women for one's entire life.

Developing self-awareness in regard to particular kinds of denial and deception is part of the educative process of every Jesuit, one hopes. For example, denial would be operative within John were he later to become acquainted with other women in a superficial way and pretend to himself and others that these relationships were friendships of any depth. Denial is also seen in celibates, single persons, and spouses who become enchanted with a person of the opposite sex, spend time with the person and think about her or him, while congratulating themselves that sexuality is not involved. In hibernation, awareness and arousal are apt to forget that spring is an inevitable season. If spring suddenly erupts, with no prior thought to its eventuality, fear may compel the one taken by surprise to lash out and reject the one seen as the harbinger or to slam the door without explaining the exit. This is sinful destruction.

Denial and deception work hand in hand when friendship is hidden by masking a friendship relationship in a "safer" designation—"we're colleagues," "it's purely pastoral," "he's tutoring me," "we work on the same projects"—because one is ashamed of one's own feelings or fears scandal.

These dangers, these denials and deceptions, these clefts and crevices in the stone, are part of the darkness and cross of friendship. In some friendships, of course, sexual attraction is minimal though affectivity has strength. In other friendships, sensual dimensions lessen as affection, through complementarity, deepens, especially if the two persons are determined to keep their primary commitments and live their lives by the intentionality of these commitments and by prayer and the presence of God, prayer and presence they willingly invite into every facet of their beings.

That suffering is inevitable in intentional friendship will not deter those who see the value and need for a witness of friendship within our Catholic community and our culture. Forbidding the emergence of sexual and openly affective oneness does not mean, however, that desire and affective love vanish within the individual man and woman. Opportunities for heartbreak abound. Great maturity combined with depth in spirituality is mandatory. For desire does not disappear overnight; fantasy does not fade in a season. No one should interpret coupling and intentional friendship as sinful over against sinless. The dynamic of friendship is not order and perfectionism. Repentance and forgiveness are the qualities that must accompany struggle with fidelity to vow and caring about others in personal love.

Affirming the separateness each is as person and navigating the shoals created by individuality can facilitate the retreats necessitated by the emergence of the erotic. It is trust, which means openness and honesty between the two persons, that allows one to call relationships friendship. Though awkward, the designation "intentional" has been deliberate. According to Rollo May intentionality implies two meanings: (1) simple future, "something will happen"; and (2) personal resolve, "I will make it happen." In other words, "we put ourselves on the line." Connecting intentionality to psychological vitality, May feels that intentionality defines the aliveness of the man or woman, the potential degree of commitment, and the capacity to deal with intensity. Or as Paul Tillich says, "Man's vitality is as great as his intentionality; they are interdependent."

Persons of Christian faith are committed to the vitality of Jesus, a vitality that has the courage to struggle with upheaval reality, a vitality that fuses struggle with love. When struggle denies love and love denies struggle, vitality and wholeheartedness disappear.

I believe that, whatever the cost to ourselves, some of us who are men and women in the Church must not be so afraid of each other that we, by distancing, or dissension, or demonic use of power, destroy each other and mutilate the Church.

I believe that, whatever the costs to ourselves, some of us who are men and women in the Church must come close enough to love one another deeply yet in that closeness sever no public or private vow. When we do this we are doing God's work in the world, especially in North America where the meaning of promise and vow needs revitalization so intensely.

If this be a salvific moment, some of us must remember that Gethsemane as well as Easter, Calvary as well as Epiphany, come with salvific moments. Those who wear the fine raiment of easy peace, be it easy sanctity or easy values, live in the emperor's palace, not the Lord's.

Difficulties in
Celibate Love

CHRISTOPHER KIESLING, O.P.

LOVE BETWEEN WOMAN AND MAN begets much joy
as it develops, but it also brings much suffering. People often find it too difficult to meet the demands which that
kind of love makes upon them. The failure of so many
marriages, both those which are simply unhappy as well as
those which end in divorce, testifies to the difficulties of
assimilating this kind of love fully and successfully into
life. Celibates share with other men and women the hard-
ships of integrating this kind of love into life, but they also
have peculiar problems because of their celibate vocation.
In this chapter we will be reflecting on some of the difficulties, both common and particular, which celibates may
have to face if they venture upon this sort of human love.
Not every celibate will encounter every one of these trials
nor have to relate to someone who will, but it is helpful to
be aware of possibilities.

An obvious challenge to celibates in the experience of
love between woman and man is accepting the limitations
which celibacy places on that love. Initially we think of the

restrictions which celibacy imposes on the physical expression of love.

Acceptance of these limitations can be very difficult. Love between man and woman drives forcefully toward sharing genital pleasure. Generally speaking, men will feel the pressure for this satisfaction before women, though it will be felt more pervasively by women when it is felt. Younger celibates, less practiced in absolute chastity, generally will have a greater struggle than older celibates. Yet many priests and religious have an especially difficult time in the middle years.

Discipline is called for, and discipline is often painful. It is not, however, merely self-denial. It is, rather, a way of expressing love. To restrain one's desire for a physical expression of love incompatible with the loved one's celibacy (or whatever state or condition the loved one is in) shows respect for the integrity of his or her chosen way of life.

An advantage accrues to celibates in love relationships because of this limitation on physical expression: they are forced to express their love more verbally. Verbal expression is much less ambiguous than physical expressions of love. After all, what do these physical expressions mean? Do they mean "I care for you" or "I feel the urge for some sensuous pleasure right now"? "I like you because you are you" or "I like you because you give me pleasure"? Husband and wife might patch up a quarrel by making love. But do they resolve the problem which occasioned the argument? Do they know any better what thoughts and feelings are going on inside each other? It is easy to "kiss and make up" but leave smoldering embers inside to enkindle the next log thrown upon them.

A much more subtle limitation is that which must be

placed on the affection itself. Celibate love is not conjugal love minus the sharing of genital pleasure. Conjugal love is selective and exclusive. The prophets of Israel used the imagery of God as the husband of Israel to express the mystery of divine election, the fact that God had chosen Israel to be his very own people and himself to be their very own God, an exclusive relationship. Celibate love between woman and man will be selective because we do not have the psychic energy to give everybody the kind of love we are considering here. But it will be selective of more than one; it will not be exclusive, for one only. It will extend to several, though differ in its motive, intensity, and expression with each.

This limitation means that a celibate does not devote to a beloved all the time and energy which is not invested in ministry and necessary affairs of community, be it religious congregation, parish, or diocesan presbyterium. Something is awry if it can be said of a celibate: "She is always with him except when working in ministry or engaging in community business." "Unless his ministry brings him into touch with others, he is always with her."

Some celibates may have chosen celibate life precisely in order to give themselves to God in prayer more often, for longer periods, and more intensely than they would probably have given themselves if they had chosen marriage with its cares for children. If now, because of a loved one, a celibate is content with giving time and effort to prayer only in the measure he or she would have given in marriage, he or she is preventing the fulfillment of his or her own choice, perhaps even taking back from God what once was given or promised. More time and effort for God in prayer may not have been an explicit motive in choosing celibacy. Then not giving more time and energy to prayer because of a loved one is at least missing an opportunity; it surely is not meeting the expectation which the Christian community generally has of those professing evangelical chastity as a way of life.

In foregoing Christian marriage, celibates embrace a way of life which fosters charity through the development of affection which is less selective and exclusive than married love. The celibate is called from the outset to love many people, gradually learning to perceive in many the high worth of each, and so grow in the love of all men and women—the authentic counterpart of love of God. The married person grows in that love of all by perceiving the value of one and gradually of many and ultimately of all. So a celibate who focuses all her or his energies for love on one person, who gives all the time possible to one, does not appear to be approaching love between man and woman in a manner appropriate to celibacy. If, perchance, she or he seeks with the loved one a "two against the world" sort of relationship, the approach is not even in the manner proper to Christian marriage.

When we speak about celibates' having human love for many, we are not saying that they are to love a community—religious, parish, whatever—over against loving one person. A community as such is a network of relationships. What celibates are called to love is many people, not a network of relations. They are called to love the persons who are in communion. Nor are celibates to limit their love to one group of persons, as spouses limit their love to one individual. A community, that is, a group of people in communion, is not a substitute for a spouse in a celibate's life.

Celibates who experience love between woman and man will very likely at first be so fascinated by the loved one that they will be deaf to the call to give themselves generously to God in prayer and to others in human affection. When they regain their hearing, they will find it difficult to answer the call they now hear. This kind of love for this one person seems so totally satisfying! How love others too? Why love others? Yet if love is to be celibate love between man and woman and not married love minus shared bed and board, limitations on this love—not merely its expression, but the love itself—will have to be accepted. One may say that then we are no longer talking about love between man and woman. Yet we certainly are, though we admit that such love exists in very different manners in celibates and in married people.

Separation is another limitation to which celibate love between man and woman is subject. Celibate love means many wrenching good-byes that leave the spirit twisted and torn and wondering how often it can endure such torture. It means aching absences for long periods of time, perhaps with meager communication. Married people have to undergo separation from one another for various reasons, so this is not entirely the peculiar lot of celibates. Yet separation for long times at great distances can be assumed as an inevitable part of celibate love, while for the married such separation is exceptional. In any case, the celibate is usually not physically present with the beloved to the extent that a married person normally is.

Separation is painful because it strikes at the very core of a love relationship. Celibate love is a continual mutual intimate sharing, supporting, and caring between two people, in friendship with affection. It is "with affection" because the people involved are attracted to one another, like one another, are comfortable with each other, and, in the present case, precisely as man and woman. Initially this affection will be very vividly felt—romantic love; but in time it will become calm.

Celibate love is "in friendship" because it supposes

common ideas and values, not necessarily the same ones but complementary or supplementary ones, or, if contrary, then acceptable or tolerable because of those ideas or values which are in harmony. "In friendship" signifies that the couple have similar or related perspectives on life.

The activity which goes on in this milieu of affection and friendship and which constitutes the relationship as active is "sharing, supporting, and caring." "Sharing" means letting another know what is going on in one's life both externally and internally: travel, work, meetings, projects, recreation, thoughts, desires, fears, hopes, disappointments, angers, plans, pains and aches physical and mental and spiritual. This list is illustrative of the kinds of things which may be shared and does not mean everything has to be shared with everyone or anyone. The sharing is certainly more than superficial, though it may be less than totally comprehensive. "Supporting" means helping another with all that is shared, perhaps challenging it, perhaps affirming it, but always offering self as someone whom the other can lean on in need. "Caring" means being interested in what is going on in the life of the other, anticipating it, being willing to act to help with it.

This sharing, supporting, and caring is "mutual," for we are talking about a relationship in which two people are more or less equally involved. It is "intimate" sharing because it extends to what is going on inside of each person. It is not called intimate because it shares so-called intimate physical pleasures. In fact, this intimacy goes beyond sexuality to personhood, though sexuality is the avenue through which personhood is reached. Finally, it is "continual" sharing, etc. It is not continuous, for there are interludes, at least in explicit actual sharing, supporting, and caring; but these activities are frequent enough to give the people involved a sense of loving and of being loved, a sense of special affective union, a sense of living two lives rather than one.

Separation, we said, strikes a critical blow at a relationship: the people involved cannot talk together; they cannot do things together and then share their thoughts and feelings about them; they do not know much about even the external activity of one another from which they might surmise, on the basis of past experience, what is going on inside. Separation interrupts that living together which Aristotle saw as the essence of friendship (*Nichomachean Ethics,* ix, 12).

Letters and telephone calls are weak substitutes for face to face communion. If a solid basis for friendship has been laid by sufficient face to face sharing, supporting, and caring, then occasional visits together with letters and telephone calls may be sufficient to sustain an alive relationship, that is, actual sharing, supporting, and caring which are felt. But once separation occurs, if sharing and expressions of support and care become infrequent, the love relationship simply dies; another sort of relationship takes its place, one that is more superficial, less involving, less significant, more dispensable.

Strong feelings of affection may remain in one or the other or both parties after separation and a breakdown in communication. But those strong feelings of good will toward another simply feed the one who has the feelings, not the other person. These remaining feelings may be thought of as love for the other, but they exemplify St. Augustine's observation that we often love our loving more than we loved the beloved. We feel good in our affection for another and are satisfied with that; we do little or nothing to inform the other of our activities, open our inner selves to him or her, show support in his or her difficulties, give care in his or her needs; nor do we seek this sharing, support, and care from the other. A "significant other" in our life is not the same as a beloved.

Besides the limitations to be accepted, celibate love in the beginning, perhaps for a long time, and to some degree always, entails tensions to be borne, conflicts to be resolved, and hard choices to be made.

Tension, conflict, and hard choice occur between a celibate's ideals and the feelings experienced in love between woman and man. The feelings referred to here are many others besides genital pleasure. The chaste celibate at least knows what stance to take toward that pleasure, though he or she may continue to be disturbed by its occurrence, even though not directly willed. Simple sensuous pleasure may be more problematic, especially if the celibate is imbued with a spirituality that regards negatively pleasure of all kinds. The vehemence of the affection felt for another person may make the celibate wonder if she or he really does love God above all things or actually prefers a human being. When expectations are thwarted or plans fall through, feelings of disappointment will conflict with the desire of depending only on God for happiness.

Other tensions, conflicts, and difficult choices exist between the beloved on one side and, on the other, God or other people. Should time be given to enjoying and caring for the loved one or to praying before God? Is so much thought and emotion expended on the beloved a failure to love God intensely? The other pole to which the celibate is pulled may be some community. Whose needs are to be met, those of the community or those of the beloved? In satisfying the latter, are the former given the dedication they deserve? People to be served are still another pole of tension, conflict, and choice. If time is free, should it be given to the loved one or to an extra effort of ministry? The tendency of love between woman and man to exclusivity promises tension and conflict and hard choices when the celibate attempts to love other people as well as a beloved one. What of self is to be given to each? How much time? How are others not to be offended when one is preferred on a particular occasion?

Even the loved one's well-being may be pitted against itself: her or his joy is desired and worked for, yet an honest admission must be made which, though in the long run beneficial, will presently hurt. Shall silence be kept or the admission made? Painful it is also to stand by in order to let the loved one grow when that growing process means her or his suffering. Love's desire is to step in and relieve the suffering, but love's desire is also to foster growth.

Loving itself brings tensions, conflicts, and painful choices. In loving, we tend to wish a return of love. Yet to ask another for love is to ask that person to become vulnerable to the difficulties we are considering in this chapter. It is to ask another to complicate his or her life and to suffer for our sake. So the paradoxical situation arises of loving another, that is, seeking another's well-being, yet at the same time asking at least implicitly that he or she, responding with love, assume the suffering entailed in loving.

Another person may respond generously to our love and assume vulnerability, and even actual suffering, by loving us in return. Then we suffer because we realize that we cannot satisfy all the desires and expectations which are contained in the other's love. To love another, to seek another's well-being, and be aware that his or her hopes springing from the love which he or she gives in return cannot be fulfilled is another painful paradoxical situation.

Finally there are the tensions, conflicts, and hard choices between the satisfaction of our own preferences and the satisfaction of the beloved's choices. As the loved one responds to her or his call to be with God in prayer, to be with community, to give self to others in ministry and in friendship, the loving celibate has to bear the suffering of the loved one's absence, in order that the loved one may have that fulfillment which the celibate's love affirms for her or him.

Misunderstandings are also the lot of men and women who become involved in love with one another. A man and a woman may each feel a very different kind of affection for the other. One may be "in love," while the other considers herself or himself simply as a companion, coworker, associate. Objective signs of affection then carry different messages for each; the ambiguity inherent in these signs becomes apparent—but not, unfortunately, to the people involved. One interprets a kiss as a commonplace greeting and the other as a sign of special delight at being together again. Very different expectations arise. One expects the other to be at her or his side during a social gathering, but the other expects to spend most of the time with several people. The hurt, anger, annoyance, and argument which such misunderstandings can beget is easily imagined.

Even when two people have the same sort of affection for one another, misunderstandings arise. All too readily we project on another person our own experience of an encounter or of a relationship. We presume that the other person experiences the same thing in the same way we do, by and large at least, even though we admit some minor differences. We also expect the other to respond as we do. In a word, we tend to determine unilaterally the shape which the relationship will take and to dictate how the other person shall love us.

Of course this approach is both wrong and disastrous.

To interpret the other person's experience to be the same as ours is to ignore the fact that the meeting or relationship is being assimilated into a very different and indeed unique personal history, in the light of which it is being perceived and evaluated. Even though the same kind of love is experienced on each side, the way it is experienced and the assessment of it differs immensely. The responses will obviously differ also. To expect, and much more to demand, that the other respond as we do, or as we wish them to, is not only to insure misunderstanding and suffering but also to smother the love which the other would give. To be loved is a gift or it is not being loved at all. We cannot dictate a gift, what it shall be or how it shall be wrapped.

To put self in the loved one's place and see the relationship from his or her point of view is very difficult. To gain this perspective is especially difficult in early stages of a relationship because one is so caught up in the ecstasy of one's own experience. One has enough to do to assimilate into one's own personal history this encounter and relationship, determine its meaning, and assess its value. Hence all the more simple and handy is it to presume that the other person's experience is the same when in fact it differs, and to count on his or her manner of loving to be the same, only to be brutally disappointed by the discovery that it is not.

Part of personal history which determines how a relationship is experienced is a person's sex. Men and women experience love differently. Whether this difference is inherent in the nature of male and female or simply cultural is unimportant; at this time of history it is real and common. Love tends to pervade the whole of a woman's life in a way it does not the whole of a man's life. For the woman, the loved one becomes much more the center of life than for the man. As a result, the woman may think the man esteems the relationship less than she does, and the man may think the woman is smothering him in the relationship. A woman's absorption in her ministry and the people she serves tends to be more comprehensive than a man's. Therefore a male celibate may feel that his loved one does not care for him very much and she may think he expects too much personal attention.

Behind seeming harmony in living out a relationship there may lie fear of loving and being loved in one or both partners. The fearful one goes along with the conduct of the relationship while interiorly trying to cope with the uncertainty felt but incapable of being articulated. The fear may be of loving, of giving self to caring for another, because the demands which such dedication will make on his or her abilities and impose on his or her freedom are obscure or are deemed too burdensome. Or the fear may be of being loved, of being endowed with the awesome power of making another person happy or unhappy by one's own conduct. To be in such a situation means being deprived of freedom and control over one's own life. To be loved means that one's smile or frown some morning can make or break someone's happiness for a whole day. If fear is lurking underneath an otherwise apparently smoothly flowing relationship, much misunderstanding is being generated. There will be much pain when the fear expresses itself in the guise of some unconvincing rationalizations for terminating the relationship.

Some misunderstanding can be avoided by the couple's talking together about their relationship, each one attempting to articulate how he or she feels and how he or she perceives the other's feelings. But even this talk is not a guarantee against profound misunderstanding. After all, even these words are heard by each partner against a dif-

ferent background of past experience and current expectation. When one says, "I want a simple friendship," he or
she may mean by "simple friendship" something quite different from what the other person understands. Moreover, one person's expression of what he or she feels
toward the other may frighten and confuse the other. To
handle the fear and confusion, the other may retreat from
the relationship in the hope of being free from the fear
and confusion, or being able to handle them alone or with
a third person. But the retreat can cause misunderstanding
and suffering.

Finally, talk about feelings toward one another and
about the status and future of the relationship can become
an obsession. The desire and the effort to avoid or clear
up misunderstanding and to achieve clarity of mutual understanding can result in the pair's talking about almost
nothing else but their feelings toward each other and the
precise status of their friendship. The common ideas and
values which are the basis of friendship become narrowed
down to the one idea and one value of this particular
friendship. Endless hours are then spent in the impossible
task of reaching perfect agreement on that idea in the
hope of perfect agreement on its value. The friendship begins to feed upon itself. It is doomed.

Friendship needs conversation—exchange by word,
by letter, by phone—to be an actuality, but when that conversation is concerned solely or mainly with the friendship
of which it is the conversation, that friendship dies of ex-
haustion from attempting the impossible. The partners
will become greater strangers to one another and less
comfortable with one another than they were the first day
they met, when they scarcely knew one another.

Also to be reckoned with in the experience of love
between man and woman are the ugly feelings, inadequa-

cies, and questionable motives that may surface. The first ugly feeling to come forth may be envy. The celibate would like to be with, and have the attention of, the loved one. He or she sees another person enjoying the loved one's presence and attention. A sadness descends upon the celibate—a feeling of depression to the point of distraction. What is deemed another's blessing is regarded with sorrow, an attitude opposed to love of neighbor. If the envy strikes at a social gathering, paying attention to other people becomes painfully difficult; escape from the situation is sought. Attention to work can be difficult if the spirit is weighed down by the envy of another's good fortune in having the company of the loved one.

When a relationship has developed, when presence and attention have been won and are taken for granted, the celibate may one day chance upon the loved one in the company of another man or woman. Suddenly, quite irrationally, the celibate will feel a huge green monster of jealousy well up within. Someone is taking my loved one from me! Disbelief, rage, disappointment directed to the usurper, or to the loved one, or to self, consume the soul. Noble ideas about celibate love's being non-exclusive and affirming the freedom of the beloved do not prevent the feelings but only make them appear more shameful.

Passing painful moments of envy and jealousy make the celibate aware of the possessiveness in his or her love, despite self-made interpretations of that love as selfless. Envy and jealousy also point to an avaricious quality in the celibate's love. Strictly speaking, the avaricious person delights excessively in having money, not to put it to use as it is meant to be, but simply to have it. The celibate may discover a kindred inclination: he or she wants the presence, time, attention, care of the beloved, not for the sake of a richer life for self and the beloved, but simply to have them. There cannot be enough of the loved one's presence and devotion. They are fervently and cleverly sought. But it is they which are ultimately desired, sought, and enjoyed, not the welfare of the loved one.

In coping with difficulties in love such as we have been considering, the celibate will become aware of personal inadequacies. His or her ability to love unselfishly and generously will become apparent. He or she will become aware how much his or her love is need-love as opposed to gift-love. In need-love, love is given, not simply because the loved one deserves love, attention, and care, but because within self is a need, a drive indeed, to love, attend, and care. Thus the lover benefits as much as the beloved. Gift-love, on the other hand, is simply giving to another freely, without compulsion, without any inner need driving to the giving. Such love enriches, but it does not fill any holes, so to speak. It presupposes fulfillment or a willingness to forego personal fulfillment.

By gift-love the other is loved for his or her own well-being, including his or her total freedom to the point of gift-love's being happy with the beloved's growing independence and freedom from any compulsion to return love. Here, the celibate becomes aware, is the stratosphere, the high altitude, of love, touching on the divine. He or she is conscious of being very poor in the ability to love so generously and unselfishly.

Erich Fromm, in *The Art of Loving* (New York: Harper and Row, 1956), claims that if we love, love will be returned. He does not mean, of course, that if I love this particular person, he or she will necessarily return my love. But if I love people, some will return it. We do not have to love in a manipulative way in order to ensure that we receive love. We are not compelled to go in search of love and snag it somewhere. We need to love as unselfishly as we can with faith and trust in the other person that he or she will be perceptive, sensitive, courageous, and generous enough to respond in love in his or her own way. If a certain friendship is especially important to us, we have to trust God that our life is in his hands, whatever may happen to the friendship, whatever direction or shape it may take, even if not in accord with our dreams. To have such faith and trust in another person and in God, to love without counting too much on a response of love, to let go of personal dreams in order that God may make of one's life what it is to be—all that is also in the stratosphere of love; before it the celibate becomes aware of how impoverished he or she is in the ability to love.

Love which does not count on a return of love is not indifferent or passive about a response. Paradoxically, it desires a return as its consummation. It therefore leads to revealing personal life to the other, spending time with the other, sharing activities and reflection upon them, so that opportunities are provided for a return of love to emerge. But truly generous loving will not try to force that return of love to emerge or dictate when, how, or in what shape it should come forth.

Meager is the ability of most of us to love generously, desire a return, provide for it, but at the same time not force it or dictate its form. If we go out of our way for others, we tend to expect some definite response from them. When such response does not come to us in a relationship, we stop going out of our way for the other. Perhaps sometimes that is the prudent response, but sometimes it may simply reveal how poor we are when it comes to generous loving.

Not only does the celibate's love often fall short of the ideal way of loving; sometimes its motivation is questionable. In the 1960's, when priests, sisters, and brothers

were beginning to depart in large numbers from the
priestly ministry and religious life, one former priest and
sister were interviewed for a newspaper. With apparent
thrill and glee over having discovered something daring
and even naughty, they told how they used to meet in the
office after work hours to do a little "smooching." Their
manner in the interview suggested strongly that they were
experiencing a delayed adolescence, at least in the sphere
of the relation between the sexes. What may appear to be
a generous and profound love may be, alas, a rather superficial infatuation, an initial falling in love which for some
reason did not occur earlier in life. When the excitement
of the new experience wears off, little of authentic love
may be found and the friendship may vanish like smoke.

Now and then one comes across the observation that
falling in love, or being in the state of having fallen in
love, is a neurosis. The fact behind the observation is, of
course, that a man and woman "in love" are living at a
high pitch of emotion, so that their thoughts are very
much caught up in themselves, one another, and their relationship. When they peer out of their world into the
broader one, they see it through the proverbial rose-col-
ored glasses. Eventually, of course, this ecstatic state
passes. They return to a normal level of emotion and once
again deal with reality as it is. A sobering thought for celibates is to realize that perhaps what appears to be a grand
and noble love is a dose of neurosis and that, when the
dosage wears off, not very much real love will be found to
be beneath all the glorious sentiments.

Another question that can be put to a love relationship is whether it is a distraction from solving some personal problem. Is love being bestowed on another for his
or her welfare, or are emotions, thoughts, and actions cen-
tering on another person being indulged in for the pur-

pose of keeping one's mind off a personal difficulty which is calling for resolution? Or perhaps the celibate is loving someone in the expectation, perhaps subconscious, that either that love or that person is the solution to the personal problem.

Some women periodically feel a great need to be hugged—by anybody, really; they simply want to be hugged. Not a few men like a pretty face. A question that can be raised about a celibate's love is just how much of it is motivated by such sensuous needs and pleasures as the two mentioned above. The celibate has numerous needs at this level, and he or she can satisfy many of them through someone with whom familiarity is gained. We are not talking about a relationship based on satisfying the need for genital pleasure or even genitally-related sensuous pleasure, at least that which is proximately related. The love in question is one which at bottom is simply a desire for another person because that person provides satisfaction for a whole complex of sensuous needs, such as a handsome or pretty companion, someone to hug or be hugged by occasionally, a feminine or masculine voice to hear, a strong hand or a soft hand to hold. What is wanted is not the welfare of the other but one's own sensuous satisfaction. A superficial good is wanted, but it may be wanted intensely and vehemently, so that the desire for it passes as some sort of worthwhile love.

The celibate reflecting on his or her love may be able to affirm in truth that it is not simply delayed adolescence, a neurotic condition, avoiding or solving a personal problem, or the desire for sensuous pleasure. But he or she may very well discern some elements of these kinds of love cropping up from time to time, or even frequently and regularly, in an otherwise soundly growing love, not yet perfect but gradually maturing. That parting embrace the other day was really less an expression of care for the other than satisfaction of the urge to be held by someone which was felt all that day. In an adolescent way, more attention was paid in the last visit to the personal thrill of enjoying the loved one's beauty than to the concerns, hopes, and fears which she spoke about.

Celibate love may very likely be lived through in considerable darkness. The celibate will not have a very clear idea of where his or her love and the love relationship is going. A married person is in a similar situation. He or she too cannot be certain of what turn his or her love will take in a decade, how his or her spouse will love in the future, or whether the marriage will eventually prove to have been a success or failure.

The married person, however, has made a covenant with another person to aim at a fairly well defined goal. Much literature and many counselors are available to further clarify that goal and advise on how it can be reached. Society and Church provide many services to support people in their pursuit of that ideal and to hold them together when difficulties tend to separate them. But what covenant does the celibate make with the loved one? A covenant of some kind could be made, but how many ever think of it? Of course, the question arises as to what the goal of that covenant would be. Who has ever defined it? And what sort of support does either society or Church provide for celibate love if it begins to dissolve?

The result of largely negative answers to these questions is that a celibate love relationship is usually dependent almost solely on the subjective views, aspirations, and feelings of each of the partners from week to week, month to month, year to year. No common goal can be appealed to, much less a covenant to pursue that goal. No third person or community is particularly interested in the preservation of the relationship. Celibate love is generally pretty much a pure happening which may last a few years, a few decades, or a lifetime.

Greater darkness sets in as the celibate experiences changes in a love relationship. The emotional pitch of love on the celibate's side and the loved one's side, for example, sooner or later comes down to a more pedestrian level. If the celibate does not realize what is happening, or even if he or she does realize it, the relationship may appear to him or her to be dying. It becomes necessary to let go of the expectations held when emotions were strong and to become open to whatever may develop. But such openness means entering into greater darkness, for it means not only not knowing what may develop, but not counting on anything. It means becoming empty to receive whatever love is given—or none.

The darkness is still more dense when the celibate and loved one are separated. The knowledge of where the other person stands in the relationship, and hence of the health of the relationship itself, depends upon occasional, perhaps sporadic, and always imperfect means of communication, like letters. If for some reason communication lapses over a long period of time, the darkness becomes so intense that the relationship simply disappears from view entirely. The celibate is left in a quandary as to where he or she stands and what he or she should do. Has the relationship come to an end? Should he or she relegate it to past history and try to forget it? Or is this a period of testing, to determine the generosity of his or her love, so that to abandon the relationship would be failure? But what if that love is simply not wanted and will not be recognized, much less returned? The celibate may be left helpless, angry, frustrated, disappointed, in a very dark night indeed.

Many disappointments will mark the progress of celibate love, as they do the development of any love. Every celibate has peculiar needs for affection, particular dreams of the ideal friendship, special hopes that are evoked in relation to the loved one. These needs, dreams, and hopes may concern how he or she will be able to speak with the loved one; how time will be spent together, not just in general, but tomorrow; how often letters will be exchanged when apart; how much of inner life will be shared; how other people will fit into his or her life and the loved one's. As a relationship develops, many incidents will occur when specific expectations in such areas are not met. Disappointment will be the consequence. Such disappointment must be expected as two people interact in an effort to adjust their diverse needs, desires, and hopes to what they are capable of giving to one another and are willing to give. Some of these disappointments may be sharp and painful, the occasion for radical shifts in the relationship as when, to cite an already used example, the emotional intensity of the relationship tapers off.

The ultimate disappointment is, of course, unrequited love. Perhaps love is born and expressed; self is given; a return hoped for and even humbly, patiently sought; but the return never comes forth. Maybe love is returned for a time but then dies or is withdrawn. If it is withdrawn rather than merely dies, the disappointment may be more acutely painful, though less protracted. One may give of self in love and receive a response, but then discover that the response has been misinterpreted, that it is not the return of love it was thought to be. The discovery that what was thought to be there and was counted on does not exist at all is an especially devastating disappointment, a tearful lesson in—what? The difficulties and pains involved in loving and therefore the wisdom of not attempting it? That is one conclusion that can be drawn, but there is another, namely, that one still needs to grow in the spirit of poverty.

Before passing on to other considerations, a word is in order about coping with the difficulties which have been mentioned in this chapter—difficulties which have their parallels in other kinds of highly emotional relationships experienced by celibates and aspirants to celibacy. Many of these difficulties can be very devastating. Some of them can shake badly what little self-esteem we have. Others can confuse us so that we cease to be sure who we are or where we are going. Still others can steep us in depression which makes life a cumbersome burden or a bleak chore. A few may even lead us into a black moment where we glimpse from a few feet away why people jump off bridges or slash their wrists.

We should not deny these difficulties or our reactions to them when they crop up. If we do not acknowledge them, we cannot do anything about them; they will be free to make havoc of our lives. Humbling it may be to own them and to confess them to another friend, but just owning and confessing them brings relief. In addition, we may discover a happy way of handling the situation which our cleared minds can see or which a friend may suggest when we tell him or her of our plight. When the pain is acute, or when it is perhaps not acute but has endured so long that it has become wearisome to bear it any longer, the best move—for men as well as women—is to go to a friend, talk about the pain, have a good cry in his or her arms, and together discuss what might be done.

The friend does not have to be someone to whom we are especially close, but simply someone to whom we suspect we can unburden ourselves. My experience tells me that almost anybody will do from among the people we usually associate with. In an acute crisis, I would venture

approaching almost a stranger rather than waste life lug-
ging around massive pain for no purpose. Most people
will respond with compassion and try to understand. We
do not need more than that, for ultimately *we* have to cope
with the situation or solve the problem. We do not go to
others for answers, but for support in our struggle, and
few are the human beings who will not give us that. In cri-
ses of this kind we discover that there is more love and
community in the worlds in which we move than we cus-
tomarily are aware of or acknowledge.

We go not only to friends but, in prayer, to Friends—
Father, Son, and Holy Spirit. In these difficulties and our
reactions to them, our prayer is often the "not so pretty"
prayer of Job or Jeremiah. . . . In the variety of the difficulties which we have been talking about, we discover
how perfectly the psalms, especially the psalms of lamenta-
tion, have expressed the depths of the human heart in its
hurts and hopes. In prayer, we see our pain, the cause of
it, the people involved in it, the consequences of it, in a
larger context—in the range of our whole life; in the circle
of all those people who love us and whom we love, and
those people whom we serve; in the sweep of salvation
history culminating in the paschal mystery of Jesus Christ;
and finally in the light of eternity, the life of the triune
God, which is ours in Christ.

In prayer, deeper solutions to our problems emerge
than the answers to which we come through discussion
with friends or reasoning within our own minds; or at
least in prayer we see the deeper implications of what we
or friends propose. We discover the profound lessons
which Father, Son, and Holy Spirit wish to give us in order that we may love them and our neighbor better in fulfillment of our adventure of celibate life.

Celibate Genitality

WILLIAM F. KRAFT, PH.D.

"I CAN VIVIDLY RECALL when I told my parents my plans to become a religious. They said they wanted what was best for me, but they asked me if I really knew what I was doing. Like, was I really willing to give up married life, a husband and children? My sad father wondered out loud if and why celibate life was the one for me. He seemed confused and almost hurt that his daughter would voluntarily choose celibacy. And though he loves me, I think he still feels the same way. I really couldn't say much. It seemed a bit crazy to me too. I simply felt that I had a calling and that I would like religious life.

"I soon found that my decision was far from popular. My brother just shook his head in disgust and confusion, and my younger sister thought I was stupid. Some relatives gave me lukewarm approval, and others just became silent. My friends were more direct. They also said they wanted what was best for me, but pointed out all the fun and opportunities I would miss. The guy I was dating kind of knew it was coming, but he was still surprised and confused. Although I felt good about my decision, I still hurt when I think about us. But I felt that if I didn't at least give religious life a try, I would be doing myself and him an injustice. I really couldn't say much, only that I loved him but couldn't marry him.

"All that seems like a thousand years ago, but it has only been about thirteen years. Now I am thirty-four. Religious life has been good to me, and I hope I have been good to it. I think I have done some good work, and more importantly I feel I have grown closer to God and to people. But my father's haunting question comes back to me: Can and should I live a celibate life? The experts say that I am at the peak of my sexual life—and I believe them. I'm really at a loss as to what to do with my sexual feelings and fantasies. Sometimes I'm so lonely I yearn to be held and to hold a man. I have to admit that I wonder what it would be like to have sex with a man I love. I know this is contrary to my commitment. Yet, I still have yearnings to be intimate, desires to give and to be given to.

"Yes, I know the latest theories about integrating. But nobody says how. Integration is a nice word, but how in God's name do you do it? Here I am trying to lead a good religious life, and many people say that I do. I am a celibate for the Kingdom of God, but I am also sexual, very much so.

"Sometimes I get the feeling that I am the only one like me. Yet I think most of my religious sisters, if not all, more or less have the same questions as I. But we seldom if ever talk about it. Sure, sometimes we'll imply some things or a few friends will talk about it more or less, but seldom are the cards put on the table and something concrete done about it."

This sister is not peculiar or abnormal. She is a normal woman who is living a productive and good life, but her sexual life is frustrating. The meaning of sexuality in her religious life is theoretically clear but experimentally ambiguous. Although, through the years, this sister has been helped psychologically and spiritually, her sexuality has been given little recognition.

Consider this religious brother. "After twenty years of religious life, I'm kind of surprised to see that sex is a bigger problem than ever. In my first ten years or so, sex was not such a burning issue. No one seemed to talk about it much, and I didn't give it much thought either. In some ways it was kind of easier. Now it seems like the cover has been taken off sex, but what do we do with it?

"I tried masturbation and still do it sporadically. It relieves some tension, and I don't have the old superego guilt like when I was young. But, I still feel uncomfortable about it. I really don't think it helps me to make sense of sex or to grow. I wouldn't exactly brag about it, but what other way is there?

"It's not like the old days. Now there's much more opportunity, and maybe even pressure, to get involved with women. This sounds like an old question—but, how far do you go? So often my thoughts say one thing and my feelings say something else. I have certain stop signs that clearly tell me to go no farther—like genital contact. But what do I do with my feelings that urge me to go on? And there are caution signs that are less clear and just as upsetting. Like, is caressing out of bounds for a celibate? Where and when do I draw my lines and why do I draw them?

"Then there are the fantasies about being intimate with a woman. What do I do with them? I know repression is not healthy, and satisfying the urge is not exactly promoted by the Church. Seriously, I think satisfying my genital needs is not good for me and, I might add, is against my religious commitment. So, what do I do? Do I run around the block, take a cold shower, pray for the poor souls? I appreciate the values of celibacy especially

for my spiritual life. But is there a place for my sexuality
in religious life?"

This religious also questions his sexual life. Challenging and frustrating questions are voiced, but few satisfying
and chaste answers are heard. He tries to test new limits,
while frustrating confusion persists. This brother also
wants to live a chaste and celibate life, and he also wants to
make more dynamic sense of sexuality. Sexual celibacy
sounds good, but how?

In witnessing through a vowed and community life,
religious proclaim that celibate living has significant value. Celibacy in community frees them for a life of love for
self, others, and God. Religious are celibates (alone for
others) for the sake of the Kingdom of God. This may
sound and can really be beautiful, but there can be problems. Though sexuality is only one issue in celibate living,
our concern is to investigate celibate genitality from a psychological perspective. Important and necessary modes of
sexuality, such as primary (being a man or woman), affective, and esthetic sexuality, are just as or more important
than genital sexuality, but genitality often presents the
most pressing problems to religious. Acknowledging the
limits of abstracting genitality from its relation to other
modes of sexuality, I should like to focus on coping with
this one type of sexuality: genital sexuality in religious
life.

Specifically, five basic ways of dealing with celibate
genitality are briefly explored and analyzed: repression,
suppression, gratification, sublimation, and respectful integration. These words are often bandied about ambigu-
ously and ambivalently, and their basis of meaning—
drawn from the relatively amorphous state of the behavioral sciences—can add to the confusion. In fact, the basic

assumptions of some psychological approaches can contradict religious life. For instance, if the human person is assumed to act ultimately for gratification, then celibacy makes little sense. In the context of this article, these words basically refer to ways of dealing with one's genital self that involve conscious or non-conscious processes and value choices.

Genitality has probably been dissociated from spirituality more than any other kind of sexuality. For us to say, then, that genital sex is linked to and can even promote spirituality may sound strange, but it actually can. We will pursue how genitality and spirituality can be interwoven, and look at the sense and non-sense of separating genitality and spirituality. Our proposal is to explore and analyze succinctly the what, how, why, when, and consequences of repression, suppression, gratification, sublimation, and integration of genital sexuality in religious life.

GENITAL SEXUALITY

Genital sexuality refers to behavior, thoughts, fantasies, desires, and feelings that involve or promote directly or indirectly genital behavior. Genital intercourse and masturbation are two explicit forms of genital activity. Feelings and fantasies that activate genital processes are also included in genital sexuality.

Genital feelings and fantasies can occur spontaneously or can be voluntarily activated and promoted. Although people vary in genital desire according to constitution, situation, and stage and kind of development, all people, including celibate religious, experience in some way at some time genital sexuality. To be human is to be genital. This is not to say, however, that a person must behave genitally to be human, healthy, or holy. A person can be healthy without explicit genital behavior.

Nevertheless, celibacy does not expel genital needs. Religious can yearn to be genitally intimate, and this desire can be frustrating and confusing. Religious can sometimes feel incomplete or that something important is missing without genital intimacy. Wanting to be loved and to love sexually is natural. A religious may also want to be genitally intimate because he or she never experienced much intimacy with anyone on any level—including parents and friends. A person can transfer a fundamental desire to be loved into a simple desire to be genitally intimate. We will see, however, that genital satisfaction cannot answer the question of love.

It is important to acknowledge that the structure and dynamics of genitality point to more than just the couple. An authentic couple in genital relations go out to and receive each other in ways that transcend them both. Pleasure and pain, body and soul, I and thou find communion in genital love. The process of genitality also points to a third person, and any attempt to control or impede this dynamism is itself an affirmation of its existence. Genital love calls a couple to be responsible to each other and to others not just for the moment but for a lifetime.

We may sometimes forget that the celibate life simply does not offer the time and place for authentic genital love. Religious who plan genital relations, regulate the time, or hurry the experience can soon become tense and frustrated. Finding a place can also engender problems. Trying to be discreet, changing places, or visiting or meeting a person can quickly become tiring and contrived. Such scheduling militates against the rhythm and emergence of healthy sexuality. Genital love existentially calls for time, place, and permanent commitment, factors which seem to constitute a psychological description of marriage.

Also paramount to our discussion is the fact that there is no such reality as genital sexuality by itself but that genital sexuality involves an articulation of the whole person. Genitality is not exclusively a biological or physiological function. Though its physical aspect can be maximized, genitality should be an important manifestation of the whole man or woman. Thus, misusing or abusing genital sexuality violates the whole person. When a person celebrates and realizes genitality in a healthy way, it is the *person* who is celebrated and actualized.

REPRESSION

One way to cope with genital feelings is to repress them. A person who represses automatically tries to exclude certain experiences from conscious awareness. The repressing individual fools himself in two basic ways: in not being conscious of certain experiences, and in not being consciously aware of being unaware.

A religious who represses genital feelings still feels sexually but refuses to admit to the experience, and refuses to admit to his not owning up to genital feelings. This religious pretends not to be what he really is—sexual, and he pretends not to be pretending. Confusing? Yes. This is why a person who constantly represses lives in a world of pretense or of make-believe.

Repression is an unconscious process. To choose freely or consciously is contradictory to the dynamics of repression. For instance, a sister who represses her sexuality does not consciously know she is running from herself. Her sexual repression is an automatic process that happens to her. Although she may have some uneasy moments of questioning her sexual self, seldom can she allow herself to give her sexuality a thought. If her repression is blatantly pointed out to her, she will likely feel threatened and consequently become defensive. She may innocently deny, anxiously withdraw, vehemently protest, or sincerely intellectualize the truth. Whatever she does, she does not accept and affirm her sexual self.

Why does a person unconsciously and automatically expunge experiences from conscious and free awareness? Usually, such a person learns and relearns that certain experiences are "unacceptable," that they make no sense, or are bad in themselves, and consequently "no good person" would experience them. Such a person can learn early in life that if he is to keep self-esteem or to be a "loved me," certain nascent experiences must be repressed. To admit such feelings would risk rejection from others or create guilt (self-rejection).

Consider the sexually repressed sister as a child. If her parents constantly repressed sex in her life, punishing any sexual expression or discussion, she could have learned to feel that her self-esteem depended on not being sexual and thus feel compelled to repress sexuality. When sex suddenly and strongly emerged in adolescence, she might have found herself poorly prepared to integrate it within herself. Perhaps her religious formation was also a sexually repressive situation so that her violence against herself was reinforced. Such a sister would never have had the opportunity to integrate her sex. She would have learned to feel that being a good person and a religious is being non-sexual. Unknowingly this sister's sexual repression could restrict her religious life and impede opportunities for spiritual growth. For instance, solitude, which is essential to spirituality, might be minimized because the silence of solitude could facilitate listening to what a person may not want to hear—in this case, her sexuality.

Repression is costly. A person who categorically rejects a dynamic that is factually part of his or her make-up pays a price. Repression is a negative reinforcement; instead of expunging an experience, repression can increase its strength and promote pressure for expression. The ways a religious unconsciously copes with repressed sexual energy are usually not in the service of health. For instance, a sexually repressed religious may become frustrated, irritable, and angry. Or such a religious may automatically abstain from intimacy for fear of being sexually activated, and he may use celibacy to rationalize such avoidance. Or a religious may project or displace his own feelings by blaming others for immodesty, or perhaps achieve some vicarious satisfaction and shaky self-reinforcement by becoming the community "sex censor."

Whatever happens, a religious simply wastes much time and energy in trying to be what he is not. A repressed person can feel exhausted from going against the grain of existence—his freedom is curtailed and his life is violated. Actually, absolute repression of sexuality is itself unchaste because it is impure and disrespectful to oneself and to others. Such repression denies a person's embodiment, making him become a spiritual prune—dry and inert.

SUPPRESSION

Suppression is another way to deal with genitality that is similar to, yet radically different from repression. Suppression is also the checking of an experience. But! Suppression, unlike repression, incorporates conscious or free awareness of an experience that is kept from overt expression. Suppression is a "no" that is based on a more fundamental "yes." A religious who suppresses genitality first freely affirms genital feelings and chooses not to promote or act on them. The religious who suppresses sex actually expresses sex to himself and decides not to exercise overtly (to suppress) his sexual energy. Instead of being an unfree and unconscious decision, suppression is a free and often conscious decision.

Ideally, a person should admit all experiences to himself but not necessarily to others nor always act on them. A religious who feels genital should admit and affirm the experience. Such acceptance of sexuality, instead of repression, enables a religious to have more alternatives for action. Immediately or at a later time, this person may mortify, sublimate, or integrate his genital feelings.

The simple suppression of thoughts and feelings is another important alternative. For instance, pure suppression of genitality may be the most appropriate stand while studying. Part of studying is to be sufficiently disciplined to focus freely without disruptive experiences. The student or scholar may not desire or have no time to listen to and reflect on genital feelings; thus, sexuality is simply put in brackets. Or consider when a person wants to help another with a personal problem. To listen and understand, this person must suspend personal thoughts and feelings; otherwise, he listens to himself instead of to the other.

Such sexual suppression often calls for mortification—a "no" that is in the service of a "yes." Mortification, which literally means "to make death," is healthy when it is in the service of life. For instance, a religious who feels genitally toward another person may freely choose to mortify his feelings. He first says yes to or affirms the genital feelings and then says no to or mortifies actual gratification. Instead of withdrawing from himself and the other, the religious rejects or "kills" gratification but still remains present, along with his sexual feelings, to and for the other. Thus, he remains sexual, but freely refuses to engage in genital behavior. This religious might say: "Yes, I would like to be genitally intimate with you, but no, because of my other values." Such mortification is painful, but it is a death in the service of a celibate life of love.

Instead of being engaged in a world of pretense, the person who suppresses both accepts and affirms his sexuality and freely chooses to control overt genital expression. Instead of the self-rejection and negation of repression, suppression is self-affirmation and free choice that promote healthy living.

Moving from repression to suppression, however, can elicit problems for oneself and for others. During this transitional time, a person can be pressured, though not necessarily, to act in almost the opposite direction of his past repressed behavior. Consider, for instance, a religious brother who had earlier considerably repressed his genitality and now becomes consciously aware of sexuality, perhaps because of some experience with a woman, for example, in a counseling situation, or even through an emergence of his own sexuality in solitude. Whatever the cause, this brother may suddenly find himself confronted with genital feelings and fantasies. Confused with his newly emergent genital self, he may feel urged to act. Instead of being defensive about sex, he may now show apparent flexibility and vitality, wanting to talk or think about sex considerably, and feeling urged to act sexually. Since his brothers are used to him being his old "sexless" self, his new sexual self may conflict with their expectations and cause consternation. Some community members may try to pressure him to be his old self by criticizing him, by asking him what is wrong, or by alienating him. The community should be patient, understanding, just, and without being permissive, available to help during this transition period. And, as he moves out of repression, this person should strive to suppress his impulses as much as possible, to mortify, integrate, and sublimate them.

SUBLIMATION

Sublimation, another stand toward oneself, literally means to raise or elevate. Consider sublimation as redirecting energy from one activity to another that is judged to be culturally, socially, physically, functionally, esthetically, or spiritually "higher" or better. Sublimation, like suppression, is an acceptance of feelings that one does not want to express in behavior because of a conflict in values. Rather than holding in check as in suppression, a person rechannels his energy into activity.

Sublimation is a frequent and encouraged approach in dealing with genital desires. Instead of directly satisfying sexual desires, a celibate invests his genital energy in other activities that are congruent with and promote authentic religious life. Still, sublimation can be dangerous. The theory of sublimation can be based on a false philosophy of personhood that separates body and spirit, genitality and spirituality. Or, conversely, sublimation can be based on a Freudian vision of personhood that posits the main motivating force in life as pleasure, so that all behavior is ultimately in service of pleasure. Such a sublimation theory can maximize genitality and minimize spirituality. Sublimation, however, *can* be healthy and necessary.

Consider our main concern: genital sublimation in religious life. A religious can sublimate genitality by suppressing sexual feelings (which includes affirming and controlling them) and then freely choose to sublimate the sexual energy in other behavior. Instead of violating one's sexual self, a religious can invest his energy in action that promotes authentic religious living.

Perhaps more in the past than at present, one approach was to "get busy" especially in manual labor or athletics. Although this kind of simple sublimation can still be useful and helpful, there are other ways as well. Sometimes a religious can rechannel sexual energy into study or administrative work, or sublimate it in aesthetic and creative activity. Sexual energy can also be used to vitalize and increase one's concern for others. When suppressed and invested in love, genitality can promote one's religious commitment. Instead of withdrawing out of fear, the religious has the courage to suppress and sublimate sexual feeling while remaining in and promoting a relationship of love. A religious can also reinvest genital energy into the activity of prayer.

Sublimation is often spontaneous, for we cannot always suppress and then consciously choose how to sublimate. A religious who feels sexual impulses may automatically become involved in some kind of activity. Sublimation, however, can impede healthy and holy growth if based primarily or exclusively on repression.

Pseudo-sublimation, as this latter form may be expressed, is a way to relieve feelings, like frustration and irritability, that can come from repressed sexuality. For example, a religious who represses genital feelings may overeat—that is, unconsciously rechannel sexual energy into eating, an activity that eases his sexual tension. Or a religious may become overly paternal or maternal with students or patients. To sublimate sex in care for others can be positive, but when based on repression, it risks exploitation perhaps even in the name of chastity and of Christianity. And sometimes a religious may simply vent sexual frustration by becoming irritable and angry. This sublimation is "pseudo" because instead of elevating or improving the person, it can militate against healthy growth.

Healthy sublimation is actually necessary because of the limitedness of being human. Being situated in time and space, a person must choose how and where to expend his energy. One cannot do all things simultaneously. To promote certain experiences leaves less opportunity and energy for contradictory experiences. And when a religious is urged via genitality to promote behavior that is contrary to authentic religious living, the religious can freely choose to, or spontaneously sublimate, the energy for healthy and holy living. To repress, or to satisfy, genital needs uses much time and energy that could be invested in activity that promotes religious living.

GRATIFICATION

Gratification is yet another way of responding to genital needs. A religious can engage in genital behavior to reduce tension and to evoke pleasure. Acting only out of pleasure can be unhealthy or, more commonly, "not healthy"—that is, while perhaps "normal," it does not foster personal growth. This normal, physical type of sex is more or less bad because one person then treats another (or they treat each other) simply as a physical being, thus violating their integrity. They treat each other as though they were only "genital beings." Instead of integrating their genitality into their person, they identify themselves as merely genital, and this consequently lessens their dignity.

A more common motivation for gratification in a religious is loneliness. A religious may engage in genital activity to escape the pain of his or her lonely emptiness. Although this is humanly understandable, it is not healthy or good. When gratification of genitality is used to escape loneliness, there may be "fulfillment," but the fulfillment is only temporary.

An escape from other feelings like anxiety and depression can be a key motivating force for genital engagement. Genital activity can help a religious feel less anxious and more comfortable, less guilty and more affirmed, or less empty and more fulfilled. But, again, the consequences are temporary and certainly do not promote a permanent religious commitment. Psychologically, such behavior is often seen as an escape from oneself and from an opportunity to affirm and grow in one's spiritual life.

Furthermore, religious life, unlike the marital life, does not offer the commitment, time, and place that are necessary to foster healthy genital behavior. This does not mean that marriage guarantees authentic genital intercourse, but that only marriage incorporates the structures wherein such relations can occur. Nor does this mean that non-married people, religious or single, cannot have meaningful genital relations. But they can also have negative relations. Since genital sexuality calls for marital commitment, a person can soon feel cheated, frustrated, tense, unfulfilled, or resentful when this promise of love is not kept. These feelings poignantly say that genital sex without authentic marital love eventually dissipates.

Genital relations outside marriage can be considered "normal" in that such behavior is frequently practiced, socially accepted or tolerated, and in that it reduces tension and affords pleasure. But mores are not the same as morals. Genital relations for non-married people are not healthy (though not usually *un*healthy or pathological) and are not good. They do not engender and promote wholeness and holiness.

Though a religious in love may be sincerely moved toward genital love, genital behavior will violate the relationship because of the lack of commitment, time, and place that are necessary for spontaneous and healthy genitality. Genital behavior for a religious, though meaningful, remains unchaste because it militates against his or her psychological and spiritual growth. For instance, if a religious feels empty, lonely, and perhaps worthless, sometimes any kind of relationship can seem better than nothing. Or if two religious fall into an intimate friendship, they may yearn to share and affirm their love genitally. But if religious deliberately enter into relationships that explicitly foster genital sex, more particularly if they act on their genital feelings, their fulfillment is temporary and does not promote a good and whole life. Since friendship does not incorporate a marital commitment, friendship and genital behavior are incongruent. Actually, genital behavior in friendship calls for a marital commitment, or it destroys the friendship.

Similarly, masturbation is unchaste. Indeed, masturbation may be "normal" in the sense that it is socially accepted and supported, can reduce tension, and is a source of comfort. Still, this kind of genital gratification, at best, merely maintains a person. It does not promote psychospiritual growth. Masturbation may be motivated purely by genital desires, but more likely it is evoked by non-genital feelings like loneliness, boredom, and a desire for embodiment. This kind of escape from such feelings is simply not healthy and can impede spiritual growth.

RESPECTFUL INTEGRATION

Though suppression and sublimation are important and necessary, they are psychological ways of coping with genitality rather than direct ways of integrating genitality and spirituality in the person. To be sure, these psychological postures are congruent with and can foster integration, but their relation to religious growth tends to be indirect. And a danger of these approaches is to consider genital desires only in terms of physical needs that are to be suppressed or sublimated rather than repressed or satisfied. Genitality, however, can have more than only a physical meaning. It can have a more direct and positive influence on the spiritual life of religious itself. Instead of seeing sex as an enemy or impediment, a deeper challenge for the religious is to experience sex as a friend and a help in living a celibate life of love. Genitality can evoke and promote authentic integration.

To experience the whole from which the part emerges is integration. Integrating genitality means experiencing genitality as a differentiation that presupposes and reveals the whole person. Instead of taking genital feelings, fantasies, and behavior simply as physical functions, a person can listen to them as (genital) articulations that say something about self and others as integral people. A chaste person experiences the whole person who underlies or is revealed in genitality.

Respect, which literally means to see again or to take a second look, is a key to integration. A respectful person looks (in love) at genital sex as a manifestation of a whole person. Genitality becomes an invitation to see the deeper dimensions of himself and other people. Actually, genitality can help him to respect and fully appreciate people. Specifically, genitality says to him: "Stop and respect reality—take a second look at yourself and the other. Don't take people for granted." What any person "sees," however, depends on his presence to reality. Instead of dissociating genitality from personhood or seeing genitality merely as a biological function, a person can experience sex as an invitation to wholeness and holiness.

For example, an artist as artist is not likely to see a nude as a genital partner, but he is more likely to see her aesthetically. His aesthetic eyes appreciate her whole being—physically, psychologically, and spiritually. And in respecting her wholeness, he presupposes and actualizes his integrity. Likewise, an authentic celibate lover is not apt to identify himself or another person with a physical part (breasts, hips, genitals) or a function (companion, friend, lover), but is more inclined to experience these parts and functions as expressions of a whole being. This celibate's respect for the other's integrity simultaneously assumes and nourishes his own wholeness, which can appeal to the other to respond as a whole being. Such a person is chaste—without narcissism, manipulation, or exploitation. A chaste posture is a pure and integral presence to reality.

We can see that sexuality is usually a social process in that it incorporates or seeks another person in relation to oneself. The other person may be present, or be present in fantasy, or be missing—present in his or her absence. Important in our discussion is that the way a person who is sexually "around" relates to another is highly contingent on his self-respect. A person who appreciates another's wholeness affirms and manifests his own wholeness. His respectful awareness of the other's integrality presupposes and fosters his own integrity. And to experience his own sexuality as an articulation of his whole being increases the likelihood of seeing the wholeness in the sex of the other.

For various reasons, women often see more than merely physical satisfaction when they look sexually at themselves and others. Women are usually more inclined to see genital sex in light of tenderness, affection, and care, and they tend to hear more clearly the call for a permanent commitment in genitality. Of course, men can also see the depth of genitality and consequently become more sensitive to and concerned for others.

But men, at least in Western cultures, are more likely than women, though not always, to see genital desires in terms of simple satisfaction. When genital desires appeal to a man to "take a second look," what he experiences highly depends on his attitude toward the other or the same sex. For instance, is a woman simply an object for sexual satisfaction? If so, sex mainly means selfish satisfaction. Or can sexual desires help a man appreciate a woman as a *person*, as beautiful, as a mystery to behold?

Think of a religious brother who is genitally attracted to some woman's breasts. What does he experience? Does he see only or primarily breasts? If so, his experience is unchaste. It is not healthy or good, because no such reality as breasts exists, but only *a person* with breasts. He also dissociates or represses the psychological and especially spiritual dimensions of himself, and consequently treats himself as less than he really can be. He lacks respect for himself, and he can lose his integrity. He fails to appreciate his genitality as an expression of his whole being.

A healthier and holier stance would be to experience the woman and himself not only physically but also psychologically and spiritually—to experience himself and her wholly. Instead of fragmenting her being by dissociating the breasts from the person or by maximizing the meaning of pleasure, he could look at her more realistically and perhaps see her and her breasts as an expression of her womanhood, femininity, beauty, life, nurturance, care, centeredness, and so forth. He is then likely to keep and foster his integrity—to relate as a whole human being. His sexuality remains celibate and chaste, and it helps him grow in wholeness—including spiritually.

Consider sexual fantasies in the light of respectful integration. For instance, a sister may discover herself thinking or dreaming about sex. What does she experience? Does she imagine making love without weight, smell, touch, taste—a senseless love? Does she see genitals apart from the person instead of the person with genitals? How real is her sexual fantasy? Does she fantasize about making love as just one euphoric state, without limits, fears, and clumsiness? Does she want the pleasure of sex and the perfection of intimacy without the limits and responsibility of real, loving sex? Her fantasies and desires to make loving sex are natural, but she should try to keep in touch with the whole of reality.

It is important really to listen to and look at what her sexual fantasies are saying because they can tell something about herself and about her relationships with people. What kind of a person is she as contrasted with her everyday self? How does she act? What does she want? In time, this religious can discover her limits—honestly and truthfully how far she can go to learn about herself and to promote growth, not immaturity or fixation.

The ideal is to look at and listen to all sexual feelings. This does not mean that a celibate should try to generate and promote genital feelings and fantasies, but that he or she honestly and truthfully look at spontaneous feelings and fantasies to see what is really happening. Genital feelings may be giving more than only a physical message, and fantasies may reveal more than mere genitality. Respectful integration enables a person to be open to various worlds of meaning that are revealed in genitality. Because genitality is an articulation of a whole person, it can be an opportunity to learn from and about oneself, and therefore become more whole.

Genital desires may sometimes not involve another person, but simply be present—without an explicit other. Suppression or sublimation can be the most appropriate way of coping. Still, a person can even integrate these general or "a-social" sexual feelings. The crucial challenge is to respect the genital impulses and to see them as an expression of your whole being. And to look for the spiritual in the genital can help to maintain the perspective of the whole. Eventually a person can come to feel wholly at home with genitality and to experience the spirituality of sexuality.

A person, celibate or married, can refuse the call of integration and focus exclusively on the physical nature of genitality. We have seen that if this happens in a religious, he or she can experience immediate pleasure but lack permanent growth in wholeness. This person promotes superficiality rather than depth. Failing to respect the whole of reality, he or she impedes spiritual growth.

Too many religious do not believe in themselves or trust their spirituality, and consequently disassociate rather than integrate their genital sexuality. Although they do not indulge in or promote recreational or purely physical sex, they still separate spirituality and sexuality. Instead of witnessing to the unity of love and sex, they can subtly follow the culture's madness—the separation of spirituality and sexuality.

Ideally, genital sexuality should help a religious become more alive and in tune with the finer and deeper aspects of self and others. When a religious feels too afraid of or guilty about genital desires, he or she may see genitality only as a means of satisfaction or as something to over-control. The goal is to respect genitality when it emerges so the whole person can be seen and appreciated. This respectful integration is a chaste and celibate proclamation of the spirituality of genitality.

Priestly Celibacy from a Psychological Perspective

KENNETH R. MITCHELL, PH.D.

AMONG THE MANY TENSIONS which are currently putting strain on the structures of Roman Catholicism in our day, priestly celibacy seems to be occupying one of the central places. Other problems may be equally important, or theologically more engaging; but this does not subtract from the importance, particularly to the clergy themselves, of the celibacy issue.

Speculations about the meaning and the place of priestly celibacy in contemporary life come out of a variety of perspectives: historical, legal, cultural, economic, and psychological, to name but a few. The psychological perspective in particular has engaged the attention of many priests, some of whom wonder about such varied issues as homosexual implications of celibacy, the reality or unreality of choice-making, and the ability or inability of the celibate priest to experience or to transmit love. Recently, I was offered the opportunity to try to engage in some disciplined speculation about celibacy from the psy-

chological perspective. This paper marks the results of one
stage of that disciplined speculation.[1]

I have chosen, as the title of this paper indicates, to
write from a psychological point of view, with some emphasis on developmental issues. For me this means some
dependence on the work of Erik H. Erikson. Erikson's
work is so popular right now that one sometimes comes
away with the impression that he is the only psychologist
to whom pastoral theologians pay any attention. Certainly
there are others whose views are important, and who
should be influential. Erikson, however, pays attention to
developmental processes in adults as well as in children
and adolescents, and this across-the-board scope in Erikson
is quite unusual. Few other writers in the area of developmental psychology pay attention to age-specific or phase-
specific issues. Erikson does, and this makes his work
important for our concerns.

THE ISSUE OF CHOICE

As a beginning point, we may take note of one of the
most frequent arguments used to defend the present tight
link between celibacy and priesthood: the issue of choice.
The Roman Catholic priest, so the argument goes, has
made a free choice to be a priest, knowing that it was also
a choice for a celibate life. This choice has the quality of a

---

1. For thoughtful and stimulating criticism of the ideas represented here I am indebted to a number of colleagues at The Menninger
Foundation, in particular the Revs. Thomas W. Klink and Richard A.
Bollinger, and Mr. John MacGregor. I am also deeply indebted to the
priests of the Roman Catholic Archdiocese of Minneapolis-St. Paul,
both for their warm hospitality and for their friendly but challenging
response to an earlier version of this paper.

solemn promise. To mark the solemnity of the promise and its life-altering quality, the choice is sacramentalized in the sacrament of holy orders. Thus the choice for priesthood (and for celibacy as a part of priesthood) is placed on the same level of serious intention as holy matrimony, confirmation, extreme unction, and penance, all of which hinge in some central way upon the serious intent of the Christian believer.

Making the choice for holy orders (to continue the argument) is not a matter of blindly and obediently choosing between good and evil. It is, rather, a matter of choosing faithfully and knowingly between two or more goods. At this point emphasis is laid on the value both of celibacy and of marriage, sometimes in contradistinction to the subtle downgrading of marriage, with its implications of what H. Richard Niebuhr has called "Christ above culture." Emphasis is laid upon the knowing quality of the choice; the man who makes the choice must know what he is about. To protect the quality of knowing, the Roman Catholic Church has provided opportunities for those seeking ordination, as well as for those who bear ecclesiastical authority, to test the choice several times, and to retract it if that comes to seem appropriate. Only if the choice is knowing, and only if it is seen as a choice between two goods, can the choice be called free.

Since the choice is both free and solemn, the demand that priesthood no longer be linked with celibacy, when it comes some years after ordination, calls into question the seriousness of the priest's original intent. The priest appears to want things both ways. As one argument by Fr. Jerome Quinn puts it, it is as if a man were to choose knowingly to be employed as a lifeguard, but later to refuse to enter the water. He wants the job, but he also wants his personal safety, forgetting that he has already knowingly compromised his personal safety when he originally chose to be a lifeguard.[2]

I think that from a developmental point of view this whole argument is specious. In the following section I shall try to show why this is so.

THE PROBLEM OF TIMING

The basic argument is this: the choice to marry or remain single and the choice of vocation properly come in life at two quite different points in human development. Connecting the decision to become a priest and the decision for celibacy is therefore a psychological error.

The choice to become a priest is made at a wide variety of ages, but most priests report that their *effective* choice for the priesthood was made between the ages of twelve and twenty. From a developmental point of view this period is an appropriate time of life to be making such a choice. Although the choice of a vocational identity probably ought to be thought of as coming later in adolescence than does the general adoption of a personal identity, much of the work of settling on a vocational identity is adolescent work.

Not all of us can clearly and heathily make such choices in adolescence. Much evidence suggests that the struggle for a confirmed and acceptable sense of oneself is a problem in the twenties as much as in the teen years. Cartoonists such as Jules Feiffer make comic hay out of the identity struggles of the young adult. It is perhaps true that the social and economic complexity of our society

---

2. Fr. Jerome Quinn in the *Minneapolis Catholic Register,* November 14, 1969.

contributes in large measure to the delay and extension of identity struggles and their resolution. At the same time, it is still the adolescent period in life in which testing and resolving one's identity properly begins. The man who has *in principle* made the choice to be a priest between the ages of twelve and twenty has made his choice at a psychologically appropriate period.[3]

The choice to marry or not to marry belongs to another developmental stage altogether. It is a problem of intimacy more than a problem of identity. The adolescent still in the throes of identifying and solving identity problems is, in a developmental sense, incompetent to make the decision whether or not to marry. That this is true is partially borne out by the divorce rate in marriages contracted between adolescents, a rate markedly higher than the divorce rate in marriages contracted between adults. Psychologically, the point might be put in this way: it is impossible to make meaningful decisions about the intimate sharing of your physical or psychological self with another person when you have not yet discovered what or who your self is. You can't really share something that is not yet yours.

One possible meaning of the age-specific difference between the choice of a vocation and the choice for celibacy is that the vocational choice may be used by the adolescent boy to protect himself from, or prematurely to foreclose, intimacy struggles. Although intimacy struggles, as I have just said, are appropriate to the young adult period of life, they are foreshadowed in adolescence, particularly in the area of sexual identity. The fifteen-year-old who is confused or upset about his sexual identity or his

---

3. The phrase "in principle" is used here in a Tillichian sense. Tillich used the phrase to mean "in power and in beginning."

sexual feelings may opt for the priesthood precisely because a celibate life is involved, unconsciously hoping that
this early choice not to express his sexuality in marriage
will exempt him from the tough problems in intimacy and
sexuality which lie ahead. It is exactly the temporary and
unresolved quality of his current feelings about his sexual
self which makes him emotionally incompetent to make
such a decision.

Perhaps it is for reasons such as these that there has
developed in the Roman Catholic system a series of points
prior to ordination at which either the priest-to-be or the
authorities can reconsider the decision for priesthood and
celibacy. These moments of decision, however, tend to exist only *formally.* Having read dozens of priests' autobiographies, submitted by applicants for training programs at
The Menninger Foundation, I am struck by the fact that
few men, if any, find it possible to make use of such moments. While in formal terms it may be true that a man is
not allowed to move to ordination until he is in his middle
twenties, the psychologically effective choice made in adolescence has, by the time young adulthood is reached, re-
sulted in a lengthy period of seminary life which teaches
the young man to call leaving the priesthood or abandoning of intentions "failure." The priest-to-be has under his
belt by his mid-twenties an educational and emotional experience which tells him that to back out now is to confess
failure, perhaps to disobey the will of God.

In this connection I recall a young Jesuit, a man
whom I have known as trainee, counselee, and friend. Jesuit formation leaves ordination until the age of thirty-one
or thirty-two. As a member of the Society of Jesus approaches ordination both he and the Society must make
the choice. My friend had only recently been ordained,
and within a few months knew that it had been a mistake.

On the surface, it might seem as if he exercised free choice at the relatively mature age of thirty-one about priesthood and celibacy. But that is indeed on the surface. He made a good vocational choice in his teens, a choice which took him into the Society of Jesus. If newer developmental issues had not come up, he would have been a happy priest—and a good priest—for he is a talented and dedicated man. But a new developmental issue—the intimacy struggle—did come up, leaving my Jesuit friend sure that, although he did indeed have a vocation to the priesthood, he had no vocation to celibacy. By the time he discovered this—and one should remember that this discovery came at the psychologically proper time of life—the Society of Jesus and he had each invested ten or more years in each other. To refuse ordination now was to arouse deep wellsprings of guilt: guilt in connection with the Society, and guilt in connection with his family, who had been talking for ten years about their Jesuit son.

The final issue of the conflict would be interesting, but it is not centrally important. What is important is that the connection of priesthood with celibacy led to such a conflict. As the story illustrates, the one choice is properly a matter of adolescence, but the other choice is properly a matter of young adulthood. The illustration also reminds us that the apparent free choice to be ordained is emotionally no free choice at all, for the psychological freedom of the ordinand to choose not to be ordained is severely limited by emotional debts to diocese, order, and family. It has become a matter of what industrial psychologists have learned to call "management by guilt." Lest one should think that I am citing an unusual case, let me say that I find it in many versions in the autobiographies of priests which I read regularly.

Several consequences flow from this central problem,

many of which can be included under the heading of intimacy/distance problems.

INTIMACY/DISTANCE PROBLEMS

Intimacy, the emotional capacity to be comfortably close—psychologically or physically or both—to chosen others includes the capacity to remain comfortably distant, as well. One of the marks of successful resolution of intimacy problems is the capacity to remain at a physical or psychological distance from certain people, either because the situation demands it (as in pastoral counseling or psychotherapy) or because we simply do not want to be close to them (as in choosing one's friends).

Both the closeness and the distance involved in the concept of intimacy have a peculiarly *personal* quality to them. This personal quality does not inescapably mean a necessity for sexual intimacy, although deeply gratifying sexual experience is probably not achievable without the development of a capacity for personal intimacy. We should not be deceived, therefore, into thinking that without direct sexual expression the celibate person cannot achieve a capacity for intimacy. Nevertheless, my colleagues and I agree that almost every priest with whom we have worked, young or old, fleeing or staying, satisfied or dissatisfied, was in terms of psychological developmental issues, bothered more by intimacy problems than by problems of personal or vocational identity. The formation of priests—or nuns, for that matter—takes place in a curiously constricted world in which the opportunity to work out the meanings of intimacy for oneself is either distorted or totally lacking. A struggle is not a struggle if its probable outcome is a foregone conclusion. Encouraging seminarians to date is not a psychologically meaningful process if the choice to move ahead to ordination is already defined as the desirable choice.

We have had the opportunity to notice several ways in which the failure to deal adequately with intimacy issues emerges as a problem, as we have supervised more than fifty priests and nuns in training. The most striking difference between our Catholic supervisees and our Protestant ones in our training setting, for example, is that it is primarily the celibates who keep injecting personal issues into their counseling, who repeatedly become too involved with their clients, and who repeatedly withdraw from their clients when emotional warmth and closeness is called for.

Intimacy/distance problems are not necessarily to be equated with being single or being married. The problem has more to do with the style and timing of the choice, which means that the celibacy of non-clerical people—bachelors and spinsters—is significantly different from the celibacy of the priest or the nun. The celibacy of the bachelor comes out of having handled the intimacy issue in a particular way. He may have handled it well, or he may have handled it poorly, but he has not been required to foreclose the struggle.[4] The celibate priest, on the other hand, has lived in a situation which has required that he foreclose intimacy struggles prematurely.

What are the consequences or the signals of not having handled the intimacy problem? Some preliminary an-

---

4. We cannot deny, of course, that in some cases powerful figures in an adolescent boy's life, mother in particular, may make demands which are psychologically quite similar to those of the religious system, demands which require the boy, at least outwardly, to behave as if females did not exist or were not sexually attractive. In such cases the difference between mother and Mother Church is not very large.

swers have already been suggested, as when it was pointed out that in our experience the priest or nun as counselor becomes too easily involved with parishioner-clients, or withdraws abruptly when there is a need for warmth and support. Another consequence or signal is that, never having truly confronted intimacy issues, the priest's life style sometimes looks to others (and to himself) as if he were a perpetual adolescent poised on the brink of mature adulthood.

With a Sacred Heart nun in training, the issue emerged in this symbolic statement: there are young nuns and there are old nuns, but there are not many middle-aged nuns. In other words, when there exists a foreclosure of intimacy issues, the celibate sometimes looks as if he (or she) were trying to leap from the life-stage in which we search out and find our vocational identities directly to the stage in which we reach out to the next generation in love and concern for the growth and survival of individuals and the race.

Eugene Schallert, the Jesuit sociologist, reports that in a study of the problem and motivations of priests who were no longer in active ministry, one man who had begun to date told him: "When I take out girls, they sometimes complain that I am behaving as if I were fourteen years old." One interpretation of such a statement would be that the struggle to learn to be comfortably and meaningfully close to another person takes place in adolescence, no matter how long that adolescence is delayed.

THE FAMILY PARADIGM

At The Menninger Foundation we have been working toward an understanding of the family and family models. Much of this work was done in our Division of Industrial Mental Health, under the leadership of Dr. Harry Levinson, now of Harvard University. Our own Division of Religion and Psychiatry has extended Dr. Levinson's thinking into the areas of religious life. We work from some basic concepts. For example:

Every man has the possibility of having in his life three family or family-like units to which he belongs. The first is the *primary* family. Your primary family is the one in which you were born and brought up, and within which you received love, criticism, care, nurture, support, and education, at the hands of a variety of adults. The primary family is the family of infancy and childhood.

When a man marries he establishes a *secondary* family: by definition the family of which he and his wife are the heads. The secondary family could be called the reciprocal of the primary family. That is, the family which for me and my wife is our secondary family is for our children their primary family. Everyone in existence has or has had a primary family, for the primary family is not narrowly defined as a place where there is a mother and a father, but rather is functionally defined as the place where nurture and care are given, no matter of what quality.

There is also a *tertiary* family. This is not, strictly speaking, a true family, for it consists of a group of work associates. It is called a tertiary family, however, because of the many family-like qualities observed in groups of people working together within a department or section. As we study working groups we discover that they have within them dynamics which are very much like those of actual families. We characteristically, though not exclusively, treat others in our world of work as though they were "reincarnations" of the people who were important to us in our primary families. We have rather hidden expectations of our bosses and fellow workers, expectations more suited to mother, father, uncles, grandfather, siblings, and other important people.

This might mean, for example, that as a junior executive I would treat my supervisor—or the company itself!—as if he (or it) were my father. If I have what are loosely called authority hangups, they derive, in all probability, from my relationship with my father. These same hangups will be exercised in my relationships with the boss or the institution he represents. The translation to bishop or to Mother Church is not hard to make.

In sum, there are three potential kinds of families: primary, the family of childhood; secondary, the family of which I am the head; and tertiary, the family-like unit in the world of work.

The moment that we compare these basic ideas with life patterns in the Roman Catholic Church, we come up against a strange problem in the lives of celibate clergy. Whatever the strengths and weaknesses of celibate life may be, one fact is clear: the priest's secondary family is a severely altered or compromised one, as is the nun's. And this fact has consequences.

The first consequence is obvious. Many priests and nuns have been voicing it for some time. The quality of the priest's "secondary family" (with the phrase written within quotation marks to indicate that there is doubt as to its actually being a secondary family) in monastery or rectory or even in a private apartment is such that the priest is deprived of the gratifications which come from life in a secondary family, even though at the same time he is generally exempt from its responsibilities. As a matter of fact, one traditional argument for priestly celibacy is based precisely here: that the priest, in being exempt from the responsibilities of life in a secondary family, is thereby freed to deal with a wider world and its needs and demands. This is an important and often convincing argument which at times seems attractive to Protestant ministers when their family responsibilities and their ministerial responsibilities conflict. When the priest sacrifices the demands of a secondary family he is enabled to make the world of need his family, a fact which often contributes to his effectiveness.

When the priest sacrifices the demands of a secondary family and makes the world of need his family, he trades one set of responsibilities for another but does not similarly trade one set of gratifications for another. The priest, like any person engaging in one of the helping professions, is ethically bound *not* to derive from the world of need which he serves any of the gratifications of living in a secondary family: that constitutes using one's parishioners (or one's clients, or one's patients) for personal gratification. To be sure, there is a structure which is somewhat parallel to the structure of the secondary family, a structure found in monastery or rectory life, but the gratifications of life in a secondary family—sex, touch, warmth, deep personal involvement—are precisely the gratifications which cannot come in monastery or rectory life.

There is another consequence, less obvious and perhaps more ominous. It is that the priest tends to conflate secondary and tertiary family structures. I quote from an autobiographical statement written by a nun: "I sought the gratifications of family life in my religious community, and to some extent I received them. But this has complicated my work relationships with the sisters immensely."

This important and unfortunate conflation can be seen in a number of common problems. Another nun in her autobiography writes that in her early years in the convent she became somewhat dependent upon a slightly older priest who was rising in the hierarchy. As she became a mature nun, and he became a bishop, he still insisted on guiding her every footstep. He broke off the relationship abruptly when the nun finally told him that she was unable in a particular matter to accept his counsel.

Whatever else may be said of this relationship, it seems clear that Bishop X was seeking the gratification of rearing and protecting a child, and didn't know when to stop. To put it another way, he applied to someone else in his tertiary family (the world of Church work) standards and expectations which were more appropriate to secondary or even to primary family structures. In a relationship where he did not really have personal authority, his only recourse was to claim fatherly authority and to reject the nun when she wanted a different kind of relationship.

Thus, work relationship for the priest can be contaminated by the personal issues of living together, and the problems and pleasures of community life are similarly contaminated by work issues. In my research on multiple staff ministries in the Presbyterian churches,[5] I long ago discovered that one characteristic of the stable, long-term, productive multiple staff relationships was that the men in them socialized with each other very little. Their *major* social relationships were outside the staff. Even their wives, though not unfriendly with one another, chose their closer friends somewhere else than among the staff wives. But this is precisely what the priest has a hard time doing. It would be better if his contact with the parish pastor was

---

5. Kenneth R. Mitchell, *Psychological and Theological Relationships in the Multiple Staff Ministry* (Philadelphia: Westminster Press, 1966).

only on a work basis, but he is likely to live in the rectory with the parish pastor, who becomes the father of the "family."

Perhaps this would be a tolerable situation if it were not for the fact that the pleasures one gets from living in such a group are quite different from the gratifications of living in a secondary family. Take physical closeness—including sex, but also including much more than sex. The priest has much less access than the non-celibate to the many daily gratifications of touch. Almost all of the gratifications of touch—holding, caressing, bodies close together—are out of bounds in American culture except within the secondary family. I do not mean by referring to closeness and touch to sentimentalize things. I do mean that closeness and touch are psychologically significant (many psychologists argue that they are even biologically significant) and that they are lacking for the celibate.

Touch in itself is of course not dangerous, but there are no natural boundaries between erotic and non-erotic touching. So well did some of the earlier monastics know this that they put a wide variety of strictures upon personal touch. Sometimes they even added a second fence to protect the first, by forbidding monks to look at each other. Canon 35 of the Society of Jesus says: "No Jesuit shall touch another, even in jest."

All of the foregoing is important because it points to the fact that, although the priest may live in a social structure which has characteristics both of secondary and tertiary families, there are aspects of secondary family life, psychologically important aspects, which are out of bounds for priests. Furthermore the worlds of living and work are not easily separated. The tension of such living is likely to be much higher than in ordinary secondary family structures, and the loss or distortion of the secondary family structure becomes a serious problem in the priest's world of work.

TWO PROBLEMS OF "RE-ENTRY"

Abandonment of priestly celibacy means for the priest abandonment of priestly work, at least at the present. Many priests have referred to this process in my hearing as "re-entry." These several men, who have left the priesthood or who have married or both, have sometimes been able to share some of their feelings with me. Each of their experiences was unique, but some common factors did stand out. Two of them seemed particularly important.

One such problem was the unexpectedly great amount of guilt each of these men experienced in relation to his primary family. Such a man is apparently able to deal reasonably well with former parishioners, and even able to deal reasonably well with authority figures in the Church. The difficulties arise in dealing with one's own primary family. This is actually not so odd. If we follow the earlier argument that the celibate choice is made too early and at the wrong time, we might remember that Father X has never been a man in his family. He has moved rather directly from boy (non-sexual) to priest (non-sexual). In his parents' eyes, especially his mother's, he is always a non-sexual person. One of the reasons many mothers are gratified by their son's interests in the priesthood is that they know their boys will not be exercising sexuality with any other woman. But the priest who leaves and marries must face his mother's pain, if she is alive, and that pain is often partly caused by the sexualization of the priest. Boys don't have sex; neither do priests: so goes the myth. The clear re-entry of the priest into the sexual world frequently arouses guilt, anger, and resentment in his primary family. They in turn frequently try to exercise management by guilt upon him.

A second problem for the man in re-entry is the common discovery that no work really satisfies the way priestly work does. Since the call to celibate life and the call to the priesthood are psychologically quite different, it is quite possible that a man can have a vocation to the priesthood and no vocation to celibacy. One friend said, as he contemplated leaving an order for marriage: "If I don't marry her I'll always be angry with the Church for keeping me from her." I had to reply: "But if you marry her now without working through your feelings, you'll always be mad at her for taking you away from your vocation."

COMMENTS

It is not the place of this article to argue for or against celibacy in the priesthood. There are clear values to a celibate priesthood, and the fact that we have referred to them only casually does not mean they are to be discounted. There are also serious psychological problems with the forms that the celibate priesthood currently takes. Rather than advocating a yes or a no answer to the central celibacy question, it seems more appropriate to indicate some directions in which moves could be made, with the assumption that priestly celibacy in some form will be with us for a while.

First, it seems obvious that careful attention can be paid to late vocations, where the decision for priesthood may be relatively late, but where the decision for celibacy is made at a psychologically more appropriate time than is currently the pattern. My hypothesis, coming out of discussion with priests who did have later vocations than usual, is that some of the psychological problems I have discussed in this essay do lose their sting for such men.

Second, effort can be made to keep work relationships carefully separate from social relationships. Rather than being urged to keep their social life fairly well confined to their fellow priests, men should instead be urged to find a wide range of social relationships.

This might mean, third, that the rectory as a common form of living situation for the parish priest needs to have its place taken by a wide variety of living arrangements, including apartments. This is already happening in some areas.

Most importantly, however, it seems necessary to create a climate in the Roman Catholic Church in which those priests who do marry, who do give up the active ministry—perhaps only temporarily—are no longer seen as "spoiled," or as men who did not have a vocation in the first place. Whatever happens to the so-called ex-priest, it seems clear that doors must remain open, so that both he and his former colleagues in the priesthood will continue to want his priesthood to be exercised, in the hope that someday this will be possible.

PART TWO

SPIRITUAL DIMENSIONS
OF CELIBACY

Becoming a Celibate Lover

L. PATRICK CARROLL, S.J.

WE NEVER KNOW HOW we are doing at something unless we are quite sure what it is we are trying to do. That seems obvious, but for a long time in religious life we have not been very clear on what it is we aim at, what our project, outlined by the vows, proposed. Thus our evaluation of progress individually and corporately has been similarly muddled.

So often the project of poverty appeared to be to become poorer and poorer, have less and less, flee from any use of, much less dependency on material things. We can speak of simplicity of life, and rightly so, but our education, tastes, mobility, and security leave us looking, if not being, richer than most around us. If we redirect our aim to the Lukan concept of stewardship and see ourselves as keepers, rather than owners, and our vow as one that commits us to sharing life and service, our project changes. It becomes possible and, in fact, more Christian. Poverty that aims at sharing everything, rather than possessing nothing, or little, becomes a Gospel virtue and not just a discouraging task.

Something akin to this happens in the vow of chastity

or celibacy. Consciously or not, many religious seem to be trying harder and harder to love God more and more, seem to strive to be less and less involved with, responsible toward human beings. We seem in fact, sometimes, to hold an angelic rather than human ideal. With no yardstick to measure our progress, we create a false one or give in to discouragement at the inability to achieve this angelic state.

I want to suggest a way of looking at the project of celibacy, or, more precisely, the project of becoming what I would call a celibate lover, for that is what we are called to be: not just lovers, and not just celibate, but both. There is no virtue in simply being celibate, unmarried, unsexed as it were. There is deep virtue in loving, or even trying to love, as God loves us: freely, deeply, broadly, unpossessively.

When we look at our religious project, we need honestly to admit that failures can come from two directions, not just one. We can be, in a sense, too loving, or too celibate (though obviously "too loving" is a contradiction in terms). We can be too careful, too distant, too cold . . . too celibate. Or we can love unwisely, insensitively, possessively, manipulatively . . . too (falsely) loving. But we *can* fail on either side. The religious who has three pampered dogs and no friends fails to live his vow as much as the religious with a mistress, for both fail to live out the call they professed to answer. We can, then, fail in either of two directions. Just as importantly, we will fail! Only Jesus did not.

If we see our lives as aiming at becoming more and more loving, more and more celibate, and hope to become an integrated combination of both by the time of death, we see, schematically, our project. Every human being will wander from that line, being at times either too careful or too free, too intimate or too distant, too involved or too uncaring. We can manipulate the feelings of people, dominating their emotions to our own selfish or needy ends. We can also manipulate the minds of people in a feeling-less insensitivity to the freedom that is theirs to be. Both are failures.

Please note: I am not talking about loving only God in a celibate way. I am talking about loving real skin and bones, body and soul, flesh and spirit, human people—the kind Jesus asks us to love. This needs some clarification.

Many religious seem to think that they are called to love God alone, despite what the Gospels always and everywhere say. A vow to love God exclusively would be un-Christian, inhuman, and impossible. Jesus tells us, "This is my commandment, that you love one another as I have loved you" (Jn 15:12). St. John writes, "Beloved, if God so loved us, we also ought to love one another" (1 Jn 4:11). In fact, we search the New Testament in vain to find somewhere where we are asked to love God directly. Jesus and his followers continually indicate that the movement of grace is from God to us, and from us to others (not back to God).

How many try to live out their vow of celibacy by spending more and more time in prayer (not a bad thing in itself, if right-headed) trying to show God how much they love him and that they are totally his. But a Christian actually goes (or should go) to prayer *to let God love him or her.*

Read that last phrase over again; it is an important and neglected concept. We go to prayer to deepen our sense and conviction that God loves us, from which we can move, in his Spirit, toward a world that needs to experience that love incarnated in people like ourselves. Nothing in Scripture says that we show God our love for him by how often or how deeply we pray, how frequently we participate at Mass, the vigils we keep. All kinds of things indicate that we are sent to show his love for others, having first received it ourselves. So we go to prayer to know God's love for us, and we must go there honestly, deeply, often. But whether or not that prayer has been fruitful is not measured by how good it feels at the time, or by the great insights we derived, unless that feeling, that insight leads us to be a more loving presence of Jesus toward his people.

So, the project of our vow of celibacy is not just to love God and not just to stay celibate, i.e., unmarried, without intercourse. The project is to love and yet remain honest, free, mobile, able to carry the Lord's love where it is needed next and most.

Perhaps we need to be convinced that celibacy is a vow to love. Well, it is a vow of Christian women and men, after all, and Christianity itself is a baptismally based vow to love, whether celibate or not. It is, I am presuming, more important to be Christian than to be celibate. Celibacy must be a vow to love, a way, a style of loving, of witnessing to God's love.

Every Christian continues the mission of Christ, to bring liberty to captives, sight to the blind, hearing to the deaf, good news to the poor (Lk 4:18 ff). Every Christian is invited to love one's enemies, to do good to those who hate them (Lk 6:27), and to take seriously the injunction: "Be merciful, even as your Father is merciful" (Lk 6:36). We are all called to be ready to forgive and hence to be vulnerable to the failures of others, not just once or twice, or seven times, but seventy times seven times (Mt 18:21–22).

In Matthew's twenty-fifth chapter the entire basis on which our life will be evaluated is in terms of love: Did you feed, visit, clothe, love me? We know that but some-how we fail to connect it with our life of the vows. At the end of our lives, Jesus, our judge, will not (if Matthew is correct) ask whether we had sexual relations with anyone, or how many hours we prayed, or how many vows we took (though, hopefully, our answers to these questions will help us to answer positively the really important question). He will ask us whether we loved anyone.

So the vows we take, and celibacy in particular, are as valid as they free us to love, broadly, deeply, honestly those the Lord sends us.

Now it would be easier if it were true that we can love in general, but it is not, and we cannot. We could, perhaps, say with Lucy in the Peanuts cartoon: "I love mankind; it's people I can't stand." But to love really means to choose to care about individual people, men and women, good and bad, nice and not so nice. It means be-ing vulnerable to them, able to hurt them, and be hurt by them, and, more importantly, to call them to life. It means, not being afraid, "Perfect love casts out fear" (1 Jn 4:18). It does not mean that our perfect love takes away our fear, but that God's love for us makes us less and less afraid to love concrete, specific human beings. Jesus in the Gospels is portrayed as saving all people, but specifically by loving John and Martha, Mary and Lazarus, and Zac-chaeus, and me and you. He was able to change lives be-cause he cared about people. To do so he was able to be deeply hurt by them, "Could you not watch with me one hour?" (Mt 26:40), or "Judas, would you betray the Son of Man with a kiss?" (Lk 22:48).

As I write these lines I do believe deeply in what I say, but I do not want to appear to be naive. I realize that the religious who try to live this out, to love as God loves them, will encounter problems. They will need to become extremely prayerful (i.e., aware of God's deep personal love for them) if they are to truly love human beings and not try to hold on, to control, to possess, or be possessed by them. The longings of their human, sexual natures will arise, confusing good and healthy relationships. This will happen when least wanted, least expected. Because they are not Jesus, they will fail, as they try to learn to be celibate lovers. But these failures can at least be Christian failures, in the right direction, a falling forward rather than a falling back, and we can learn from them and go on.

Too often the Church, or a community within the Church, has judged and punished those human frailties occurring in the person honestly trying to learn to love, and it has not even noticed those failures of distance, coldness, and aloofness that destroy the Church and Christ's call to union so that the world can believe. We decide to expel the very apostolic young man admitting to homosexual tendencies, generally under control, and ordain men with no close friends, who, in fact, fear intimacy.

In every generation of religious life there have been too many crusty bachelors and mean old maids masquerading as celibates, going to their graves without once letting sex rear its head. Too often love was squelched in the process, and they witnessed to nothing but will power. What the world needs, the witness we are called to place alongside the sacramental witness of committed married love, is that there is a human possibility of loving and not having to possess or be possessed, a human possibility of loving and not holding on or being held on to. We are called to witness to a love that is one facet of the love of God for his people, a love that moves over rich and poor alike, over the beautiful people and the not so beautiful, over the alive and the not so alive.

I do not want to minimize the risk involved in living

such a project. We risk involvement and pain, risk even sin and separation from our community or priesthood, risk, in myriad ways, the cross. But I would emphasize that the risk involved in any other project is perhaps more grave. For it is the risk to fail to be a Christian, to fail to love at all. As John Courtney Murray pointed out many years ago, in choosing not to love anyone particularly, personally, uniquely, we risk never loving at all, never being alive at all, never letting Jesus be alive in us.

Let me emphasize a point already made. No one can fulfill in any successful way the project of becoming a celibate lover without a deep, enduring life of prayer. No one can reach out in an effort to really care for other human beings unless they know day in and day out how cared for they are themselves. It is only since God first loved us that we can try to love one another in his fashion. We cannot become celibate lovers if we are trying to make up for the absence of this love of God for us by the multiplicity or depth of our relationships with others. We cannot give what we do not have.

Finally, celibacy is a vow that only becomes Christian, only ultimately is possible within a community. A religious promises to support others in their project, and to accept, even to demand support for himself or herself. How often it is sadly the case that a religious struggling to love and yet be integrated within an overall commitment finds himself or herself isolated from or judged by the community. How often we fail to reach out a hand to someone hurting, believing it to be none of our business? How frequently has every community talked at meetings of other things?

We talk, for example, endlessly about poverty: simplicity of life, personal budget, personal or communal lifestyle concerning clothes, travel, or recreation. And we easily and often discuss and debate the obedience involved in a discernment process, in corporate versus personal apostolate, our mission from Church and community. And these are good things to discuss. But how rarely we talk about our corporate struggle to become celibate lovers. This struggle rarely surfaces except between intimate friends. Generally we bury our fears or temptations, failures and successes, and struggle on alone. Too often we seem to be the only one struggling while the dimming vision seems unique. We search out a director to do what our next door neighbor could better accomplish if only she were not afraid, or he were more sensitive, if only they would listen, care, share their own bent or broken dreams. In fact, it seems to me that the possibility of living out a loving celibacy is in direct proportion to a community's ability to talk openly about the subject. How few communities provide such support!

My point in all of this is simply to insist that the vow of celibacy is a part of the overall communal commitment and communal project. Our convents, rectories, religious houses must be homes where brothers and sisters challenge each other to laughter and to love, where failures are accepted and hope is nourished. The witness we give is given together, founded on the great love God has, not just for me, but for us, from which we turn together from a deeply shared life to a work of service together.

I began by saying that we can never know how we are doing unless we are clear on what it is we are trying to do. I suggest that this chapter indicates a neglected part of that project. If we agreed and helped each other along the path, all of us who seriously try to be religious men or women could better distinguish than we have been able to do in a long time how we are progressing.

Becoming What
All People Are

KEITH CLARK, O.F.M., CAP.

"I FAIL TO UNDERSTAND how God could give you a penis which is horny 360 days a year and still give you the idea you are called to a celibate life," he said in response to my question about what other things preoccupied him. "And it's not just a matter of being horny in that physical sense, but also in terms of intimacy and relationship, acceptance and the need for affection."

The questioner was a 25-year-old religious brother who knows that in a year or so he will be thinking seriously about making final profession in a celibate religious community. Our conversation took place on Friday, I believe.

On Sunday I was visiting a priest with a life commitment to religious life. He had been wrestling with the same sort of question for the previous six or eight months—ever since he had fallen in love with a very wonderful woman—and he was arriving at some answers to his question.

"I learned something from Barney Miller a couple of weeks ago," he said, "and I'd like to share it with you."

119

He described the episode on the weekly television series. One of the policemen in Barney Miller's precinct had shot and killed a man in the line of duty, and he was disconsolate. As always, most of the episode took place in the office in precinct headquarters, and it centered around this man's dealing with his dismay that he had killed someone. Other members of the force tried in a variety of ways to help the officer get over his depression. Some passed it off with attempts at humor in an effort to cheer him up. Others philosophized about it. Some in a more hard-nosed fashion just urged him to get on with life. No one was able to help.

My friend narrated the closing scene in the episode. Barney had gone to the apartment of the officer to offer some encouragement. As he was about to leave, he turned to the policeman and said, "Did you know that the largest mammal in the world is the sperm whale?"

"No," the officer responded, looking a little puzzled.

"Do you know how large its throat is?"

"No."

Lifting his arm and holding his thumb and index finger about two inches apart, he said, "About this big."

"Oh."

"And do you know why that is?"

"No."

"Because that's the way it is, and there's nothing you can do about it!"

On Monday I shared the Barney Miller story with the brother with whom I had had the Friday conversation. In his question about being "horny" there is an assumption that things should be otherwise, or that he should be able to understand why things are the way they are, or that he should be able to do something about it. In fact that's just the way it is and there's nothing he can do about it.

I knew even then that if I ever did write a book about the celibate life, I'd try to take that brother's honest question very seriously, because I'm sure he's not the only celibate person whose question veils some assumptions about celibate life. I lived most of my life with those same assumptions. If it weren't for the grace of having a good number of healthy celibate people share their own questions and experiences with me these past dozen years, I'm pretty sure I'd still have the same assumptions. After these years of listening to others, I sometimes feel as if I am a broker of other people's experiences. Having heard their stories and having had the chance to compare their experiences with my own, I now conclude that the only reasonable answer to some of the questions is: "Because that's the way it is and there's nothing you can do about it."

Often the questions center on people's experience of simply having a body and being sexual. These are not at all connected with the fact that the person has made or is thinking of making a commitment to celibate life; they are questions born, for the most part, out of the normal human curiosity about one's own and other people's sexuality.

There is a practice among most adolescents that has become almost an accepted custom and ritual. People who are discovering the physical, emotional, personal and relational aspects of their awakening and growing sexuality almost always speak about it with their peers. They are driven to do so by a very normal sexual curiosity. But practically no one enters those conversations with any willingness to reveal that he or she is seeking information and perspective. They all act as if they are experienced and knowledgeable as they share their real or imagined "wisdom."

In growing up I was not, of course, in on all the "girl

talk" about awakening sexuality, so I don't know about that. But the "boy talk" was always done with the minimum of words and the maximum of knowing glances. We shared our considerable ignorance with each other and returned to our private corners of the world to try to make sense out of what we had found out about ourselves and our friends. Each one of us, I'm sure, felt that he was the only one who really didn't know. It seemed never to occur to us that maybe the others had lied too!

I first discovered that I could use my penis for something other than going to the bathroom while I was quite young. It was a fascinating experience. I couldn't imagine why I was responding the way I was to certain stimuli, or why I suddenly had such curiosity about my own and other people's bodies. But as the other kids in the neighborhood—somewhat older than I was—introduced me to strip poker, and as we played spin the bottle on front sidewalks, I pretended that I knew all about sex and acted as if I were perfectly comfortable with my body.

Gradually I got to be familiar with my own sexual responsiveness. Our group of guys swapped stories—again, mostly lies and false impressions—about our new experience of being a man. But just knowing how I responded didn't help me know whether or not that was the way I "should" respond. And I never knew if the way I experienced being me was anything like the way other guys experienced being them. And so I never knew if I was normal or not. Some in our group were probably "turned on" by guys, but of course peer pressure kept them from ever exploring their experience. Over the years I have learned that at least I was normal in how I went about seeking to answer my questions. None of us simply asked for information from someone who could provide us with answers. We sought information while pretending we were not in need of it.

I found that in late adolescence and early adulthood the same basic pattern remains, even with the passing of generations. I remember my own embarrassment when I introduced a course on sexuality into the novitiate program. I felt sure that those novices of a new generation were much more informed than I had been at their age— maybe even more informed than I was at age 32. But I was determined not to presume anything. Experience had taught me at least that much. I had learned, for example, because I knew a man who as a novice had spoken with his spiritual director about his problem of masturbation. Two years later he confided to me that he had just discovered how to masturbate! Neither his spiritual director nor I will ever know what it was he struggled with during novitiate!

So we introduced "Clark's Fantastic Sex Course" into the novitiate curriculum. And despite my fear that I might be embarrassed by teaching things which were "old hat," I was determined to presume nothing. I even got used to the idea that they would all be sitting there *looking* like everything they were hearing was "old hat." But each year I found that I had presumed a lot. Even when novices started coming to novitiate after two, three or four years of college, and after paring my sex course down to more and more basic information, I found I still sometimes presumed that the guys had more correct information than they actually did.

I have now discovered that the confident exchange of ignorance is not only an adolescent phenomenon. People my age are not much better at sharing with one another their wonders and doubts and their experience of being sexual. On these they remain silent. Like adolescents, I suspect that adults continue the bravado of false impressions, the all-knowingness of misinformation.

By middle age we all have become very familiar with our own idiosyncratic sexual responsiveness. If we can bring ourselves to share our questions and doubts with a caring friend, we may find that we become more comfortable with ourselves. I have found that it is entirely possible for me to listen to others explore their experience and become more comfortable about themselves, even in an area where I myself am still uncomfortable. The increase of comfort and understanding comes, I suspect, from our mutual sharing of the experience, rather than from any information I have to offer.

And so, the assumptions underlying many of our questions are allowed to continue. We still say: "It shouldn't be this way. We should be able to understand why it is the way it is. We should be able to do something about it." All false assumptions!

The 25-year-old religious brother with his preoccupations about his own experience of having a body and of being sexually responsive is simply experiencing being what all people are. To be sure, the degree of comfort varies not only from one individual to another but for the same individual from one period of his or her life to another. We can almost always surprise ourselves. I am not totally comfortable with my sexuality, and I don't expect to be until shortly after they have carried me in my coffin into church. Some considerable degree of comfort is normal for mature people, but our physical responsiveness to varying stimuli, our fantasies, even our impulses and actions, will predictably startle us from time to time. To be comfortable with one's sexuality does not mean that the mystery has gone from it forever.

I think that there must be a lot of younger people in seminaries and houses of men and women religious like that 25-year-old religious brother, people asking how it is possible for God to make them the way they are and still give them the idea that they are called to a celibate life. The demeanor and discussions of the older, more established members of the seminaries and religious communities offer little evidence to suggest that they have any experience of being sexual creatures. And so the younger people understandably wonder about their fitness for the priesthood or religious life. And if they leave the seminary or religious life, they are convinced they left "because of celibacy," when in fact they may have left because they had no help in becoming what all people are.

It is not only on the level of bodily and physical sexual responsiveness that there is something to be learned by trying to have in ourselves that mind which was in Christ Jesus:

> Though he was in the form of God,
>   he did not deem equality with God
>   something to be grasped at.
> Rather, he emptied himself
>   and took the form of a slave,
>   being born in the likeness of men.
> He was known to be of human estate . . . (*Phil 2:6–8*)

We can learn something for ourselves on the level of our relational, affectional and personal intimacy needs, too.

But here too there are some obstacles. Our Church, our society and most individuals in both of these groups tend to look upon the celibate life and those who embrace it as something superior to the rest of society's and the Church's institutions and individuals.

Our Church, consciously and deliberately at times, and at other times in the manner of an unconscious prejudice, tends to regard celibacy as a superior call and those who respond to it as somehow superior to those who respond to different calls.

Many people tend to regard any attempt at a lifelong celibate commitment as foolhardy—something beyond the realm of the average human being—and they are so suspicious of the claim that they usually will not believe it. If someone who claims to have made and lived such a commitment is credible enough that people in our society can believe it, that person is looked upon often as somehow superhuman.

What is true of our Church and our society generally is echoed in the attitudes of individuals in the Church and society and by groups and institutions within the Church and society. I find that married spirituality, for instance, is taken generally as an adjunct to the life of married couples, an adjunct derived from celibate spirituality and directed by celibates. I don't mean simply that married and single people look to celibates to gain from their perspective; I am referring to what seems to me to be an assumption that celibate spirituality is the model of all spirituality, and married or single spirituality is necessarily second-best and really not so spiritual. I'm suggesting that people in our Church and society at large bombard the celibate person with an assumption that he or she is beyond or above the realm of normal human beings. It shows up in the sometimes stated, sometimes assumed attitude that a celibate commitment is more difficult, more sublime, more precarious than other life commitments.

A difficulty which falls to celibates because of the assumption that they are superior is the danger that they will be led to deny the humanity they have in common with other people. And if the denial is made, celibate men and women will be surprised when they find within themselves the same "stuff" which all people find within themselves. Their surprise will lead them to repress their humanity when they do begin to discover it, or to think that they were never called to a celibate life because they come to know, at last, that they are what all people are.

The assumption that celibate people are a cut above ordinary human beings is instilled in people while they are still very young. I can remember talking to a young man in high school and speaking with him again when he was in college. Religious life appealed to him because of the religious men he had come to know while growing up. And I thought he was the kind of man I would most want to see consider religious life. But because he knew of his own physical and emotional experience of being sexual, he was unable to seriously consider the possibility of a celibate lifestyle. He presumed that since he knew he was "horny" often and had fallen in love with several girls during high school and college, the priesthood or religious life could not be for him. The assumption: People called to a celibate life are "above all that."

I am one of the millions of people who bought and read the novel *The Thornbirds*. In the book there is a central character whose name is Ralph. When we first meet him he is a priest in a little town in Australia. He becomes a bishop, an archbishop and a cardinal. He is a marvelous man in so many ways, and I liked him from the start. But I always cringed, as I read the book, when Ralph would tell himself that he was before everything else a priest; only after that was he a man. He eventually proved that that wasn't so; he has a son, who he doesn't even know exists. The woman who bore his son never told him, and because she had a husband, the son's identity could be successfully concealed, even from the son. The young man eventually decides to study for the priesthood, and he is sent to Rome to study—to Rome where his father is a ranking member of the papal curia. Somehow or other the seminarian comes to have an interview with the cardinal, his father, as part of his examination for candidacy for orders. The cardinal asks the lad if he knows what he is getting into by taking on the responsibility of a celibate life. The lad says he does. The cardinal, although he does not know that he is speaking with his own son, sees in the boy a lot of himself, and drawing on what he knows of himself, he questions the 19-year-old about human weakness. The boy responds, "But, Your Eminence, I'm a man first, and only then a priest." Now, in the wisdom of his increased age, the cardinal recognizes that with this humble realization the boy is better equipped to vow celibacy than the cardinal had been when he denied or belittled his humanity. And everything inside of me said, "The woman who wrote this book really does understand that celibate people are made of the same stuff everyone else is."

Another danger I see in the assumption that a celibate is superior to other people is this: Celibate people will neglect and perhaps even reject as unnecessary or unworthy of them all those normal human gestures of affection and appreciation which come to them. They will brush off expressions of gratitude and appreciation. They will ignore them and pretend even to themselves that they are unaffected by such praise or applause, and that they should be "above all that."

I suspect this second danger plays on the individual celibate man or woman in some subtle but devastating ways. It is the equivalent of starving one's self of the nourishment required for human life. If a celibate ignores or denies the kind of human esteem which meets our normal intimacy needs in ordinary ways, is it surprising that our human needs heighten to the point that we eventually begin to steal from sources not legitimate for us the kind of affection we crave? Eventually we may even "smash the bakery window" in search of a supposedly unlimited supply of what we have lived without for so long.

At the point of starvation, the danger I mentioned first—the failure to recognize that celibate people are what all people are—comes back into play. Because of the feeling of starving to death emotionally, we suspect we weren't called to a celibate commitment in the first place, and so "stealing" or "breaking into the bakery" is somehow permissible. And if it is permissible, those who will not permit it to us are obviously unfeeling and lack understanding. How else could they continue to require of us faithfulness to the commitment we made without knowing really who we were?

At the point of emotional starvation we readily admit that we *are* what all people are, and that we need affection like everyone else. But we will perhaps perpetuate the assumption that celibate people—people *truly* called to that lifestyle—are in some way superior to the rest of us. The dynamic of superiority is subtle, but I suspect it is operative on almost all levels of Church and society. And I suspect it is operating to everyone's disadvantage.

I doubt if decrees or assertions from Church and society can possibly counteract this prevailing assumption. It is only people with celibate commitments who can interject a contradicting voice. And even these celibate men and women cannot speak constructively to their world with mere words of protestation. Nor can they challenge the assertion of their superiority by deliberately "acting shamelessly" or in "getting down there with the rest of the folks." I think celibate people have sometimes hurt themselves by challenging the assumption of their own superiority through their *deliberate efforts* to prove by their actions that they are just like everyone else.

If a corrective statement is to be made, it can be made only by the living witness to this truth, that celibate men and women are human beings. It is only by force of their own experience of being who they are, and not by trying to *prove* something, that the assumption of their superiority can be significantly and constructively altered. Jesus didn't set out to prove something about being what all people are. He simply lived that way. And in so doing it is true that he offended some who thought no one ought to be so clearly known to be of human estate.

If as celibate men and women we can recognize that we are indeed what all people are and accept *without demanding* the affective and intimate expressions which come to us from others, we will be making a contribution toward correcting the prevailing assumptions. If we allow people to know that our human needs have been met by the appreciation, affirmation and affection they have freely offered, then we are acknowledging our needs. We are saying that we are what all people are. But if we let our needs be known by *demanding* that they be met, we will frighten off those who will wonder if they have the resources to provide us with what we need. Perhaps worse yet, if we insist on remaining hard-nosed, dedicated people who show no signs of needing or appreciating what others give us, we will be starving ourselves, and we will be telling others that celibate people are "above all that."

It is one thing to tell someone we need intimacy and affection. It is quite another thing to acknowledge graciously that someone's sharing of his or her life, expression of gratitude or offer of affection is recognized, accepted and appreciated. It is one thing to *demand* that someone listen to me because "I have needs too"; it is quite another thing to *thank* someone sincerely for having listened.

I, a celibate person, am what all people are. If I mistakenly think that I have some superhuman ability to continually meet other people's needs, I delude myself. My commitment to a celibate life does not even mean I should have this ability to equal God in giving to others without the need to receive from them. If I recognize my inability to always provide a listening ear, sympathetic word, affectionate reassurance, appreciative glance, supportive stance, graceful gesture, without receiving the same from others, I have discovered what it takes to live in this human estate. In recognizing my capacity to give to others and my need to receive from them, I have discovered that others have the capacity to meet my needs. I make this acknowledgement by graciously receiving what is freely offered.

At times I will have to live without having my needs met. At times I will be invited to enter fully and vulnerably into life's moments of loneliness because I have a commitment to stand ready to do so. At times what I know I need is simply not going to be available from other human beings. And at those times I can rediscover the radical all-sufficiency of God. By their commitment to stand ready to enter fully and vulnerably into life's moments of intimacy, others have secured for themselves at least the possibility of a lasting source of reciprocal human love. I have not chosen that life, but my commitment to celibacy does not mean that I am called to walk blithely through life, passing up those things which are freely offered and which do in fact feel good because they meet my needs.

I think the gracious flow of affection, appreciation, gratitude and affirmation is what is expected of people who do not have a celibate commitment. The give-and-take of such intimate relationships is presumed. I believe that most people recognize that such vulnerable and transparent presence of people to one another can lead to ongoing commitments to one another. And such relating can lead to romantic intimacy and eventually to mutual emotional dependence and to making genital-sexual commitments. But I fear that some think that such a development is not only *normal,* but that it is also *inevitable.*

I have a friend who has often said that we used to watch the boy-meets-girl scene in a movie and wonder *if* they would go to bed together; nowadays we wonder only *when* they will go to bed together. There seems to have been a shift in our expectations about how intimate relationships develop. People used to recognize that intimacy *could* develop into romance, which in turn could lead one to make genital-sexual commitments to another. Now such development seems inevitable. And I think this sense of inevitability contributes to making celibate people shy away from normal intimate relationships in fear that they must necessarily lead to romantic intimacy. Maybe it would be better, some tell themselves, to ignore or deny the normal intimacy needs and to avoid altogether the normal ways they can be met, rather than get into a situation which will inevitably lead to romantic pursuits.

I recognize that one of the normal outcomes of becoming increasingly transparent and vulnerable to another is to become romantically involved and eventually to make sexual and genital commitments. But I resent the implication that what is normal is also inevitable.

All commitments evolve. This is true of the commitment to a lifelong style of living, be it married, single or celibate. But to think that because there is a normal evolutionary process to every commitment means that there is a path leading inevitably to each commitment bothers me.

I suspect that *romantic* intimacy will lead to marriage with a force that seems to approximate inevitability. But romantic intimacy is already sexual in a way that invites emotional and genital commitments. But all intimacy is not romantic.

Many religious and priests with a celibate commitment have discovered their capacity for intimacy and their need for it, but some of them have refused to acknowledge that they have that need and capacity fearing that they will inevitably be led into romantic intimacy. Then, if they finally do acknowledge that the capacity and the need are there, they may begin to allow a commitment to *romantic* intimacy to evolve, believing that the normal process they are experiencing is also inevitable.

People have forgotten that they have some control over what they will do with their needs and capacities regarding intimacy. They cannot control the fact that they have them, but they can control the expression of them. My own celibate commitment evolved over the course of many years. Having now made the deliberate choice and commitment to what evolved, I believe that part of it is to keep contrary commitments from evolving. To discover continually that I am what all people are does not mean that I must do what most people do. To discover continually that I am sexual and that I have a capacity for romantic love does not mean that I will inevitably pursue romantic intimate relationships. Having come to know that I am what all people are, I need to have in myself again the mind that was in Christ Jesus, who

> Though he was in the form of God,
> . . . did not deem equality with God
> something to be grasped at.

Rather, he emptied himself
    and took the form of a slave,
    being born in the likeness of men.
He was known to be of human estate . . . (*Phil 2:6–8*).

And being what all people are, he was humbler still, *even to accepting death.*

Intimacy is not inevitably romantic and romantic intimacy need not inevitably be pursued. There is the possibility of mortification and the invitation to accept even death. But if the need for intimacy inevitably led to romantic intimacy, and if romantic intimacy inevitably led to emotional dependence and genital commitments, then it would be true that only someone who is more than human (or less than human) could make a commitment to celibate life.

To be committed to a celibate life does not mean that one is superior to other human beings. To recognize that one is put together in just the same way that all people are does not mean that one is not called to a life of celibacy. Celibate people are what all people are, and that's just the way it is and there's nothing you can do about it!

Thank you, Barney Miller!

A Priest's Thoughts on
His Own Celibacy

PATRICK J. CONNOLLY

I BECAME A PRIEST in St. Peter's Basilica on the first day of winter just over twelve years ago. I am thirty-seven years old and am supposed to be entering my "midlife crisis" as an American male. This is what the psychological literature suggests. I was in the active ministry one week when Pope Paul VI decreed on birth control and a lot of what I knew in the Catholic Church went upside down. Whatever a "normal" priesthood may mean, I have not experienced it first-hand.

Although I keep hearing that holy orders should not be identified with celibacy, I don't see too many non-aligned celibates walking about. I probably wouldn't have given celibacy a second thought (as most people haven't) had not the Church been there telling me that it was a prerequisite for my ordination. In the old days it was looked upon as something bordering on the heroic. Today I sense that people see it more as an affliction.

Several years ago one of my students gave me a big red and white metal button with the words "CHASTE MAKES WASTE." We laughed about it in class—it was

135

meant in a light-hearted way. But beneath the surface was always the query: "Father, you seem so normal—not the kind of person who would want to be a priest." The celibacy question was always close behind.

When I decided to give the seminary a try at age eighteen, celibacy didn't seem like much of a challenge to me. I believed that my libido could be sublimated for the "loftier" things of this life. Celibacy in those days was an ideal. But like any life choice, a person becomes his decision only as he chooses to live it. I honestly wonder how many who haven't had to meet this kind of a decision day in and day out could ever possibly perceive its symbolic spiritual value. It has taken me a number of years to realize what I've gotten myself into. It makes some sense for me, but I don't think it does for too many others.

Most of my friends have left the priesthood—in the late 1960's and early 1970's. They all married. When each one chose to leave I experienced deep loss, and a lot more anger than I could admit to at the time. I was just about ready to begin believing that they knew something I didn't know. Was I going to become a shipwrecked human not fulfilling all of my potential?

I don't try to second-guess their decisions. What I do question is my own: Why do I stay? I don't think I am any more virtuous than those who have left and I don't think I am any less fulfilled. But why do I stay? I don't relish being a member of a highly visible and very unusual minority, though that goes with the job.

These past twelve years have not been terribly happy years, but they have been filled with life and meaning. Last year I was writing Christmas cards and it only then occurred to me that I was ordained on the first day of winter. It has been a winter priesthood—a priesthood closed in near the hearth, not in the sunny freshness of the meadow.

Several months before I was ordained I asked a priest from my diocese—his name was Harry—when he had decided to become a priest. "Five years after I was ordained," was his reply. His answer took me by surprise. He had a sense of honest wonderment about his living that was attractive, and he was just about to begin his twenty-fifth year in the ministry.

The thought of Harry reminds me so much of a quote that I came across years ago in college, whose author I can't recall: "God is the partner of your most intimate soliloquies. Whenever you are talking to yourself in utmost sincerity and ultimate solitude—he to whom you are addressing yourself may justifiably be called God."

Harry's ways seemed to fit that approach at the time I met him. Part of his appeal had to do with the time in my life when we met. I was searching for someone in the Catholic bureaucracy who had explicitly chosen Catholicism as a way of life, and who was also comfortable with ambiguity—someone who was able to deal with the mystery of limitlessness within his own limits. Harry knew his space, so he freely accommodated mine. I felt free in his presence, trusting that he knew what life was for.

As I look back on it eleven years later I now see that he was the reflection of my own interior rumblings. It wasn't Harry who had the answers. What began with a touch of outward rebelliousness in those early years mellowed itself into an inner journey. His special presence offered me freedom, and after having wrestled with freedom for all of these years I'm beginning to appreciate what a marvelous, subtle and inner gift it really is.

If the Christian message is going to make any sense to

young people today, it is going to need more Harrys. I've been talking about him in the past tense because a year after I was ordained his heart stopped in his sleep. I lost a mentor. There hasn't been one since, and I don't think there will ever be again.

No arguments for celibacy have ever made much sense to me over my years of priesthood because there is still the stuff of loneliness to endure—a realm not open to argument. I have no edge on the experience of loneliness, but there is a perspective of which I am becoming conscious because I am a celibate.

I read recently that it is within the very experience of loneliness that a celibate is called to bear witness to the belief that there is a Love beyond all loves which can suffice absolutely. That takes faith! I don't think too many people would choose to buy into that kind of a commitment.

At thirty-seven I find myself sometimes a reluctant witness. But as I begin entering into my loneliness celibacy is starting to make some sense to me. It has been during these past twelve years that I have been discovering along the way—hesitatingly—that the essence of my loneliness is not just crushing darkness and the taste of my heartbeat—for indeed there have been those terrifying and fathomless moments.

My loneliness has a "voice." There is a Presence within the void. Deep friendships have brought me to this, and the inevitable good-byes. I meet my loneliness. And I learn that nothing else remains to be discovered except compassion.

There are times in my preaching when I can hear a pin drop—when I begin talking about loneliness—and I sense the congregation is alive and alert and ready to journey with me.

One of the most warming experiences I've ever had was receiving a Christmas card two years ago from a parishioner and a mother of eight: "Thank you, Father," she wrote, "for helping us enter into areas where we ourselves would fear to venture alone. Your sermons are topics of much discussion around our family table."

I see my job as touching upon my own loneliness—entering into it—and coming out to describe what I have encountered. I can't make it happen for others—but I can be present during their entry into that mostly uncharted territory. I find this exciting—for it touches on the raw reality and deepest rumblings of the human spirit.

All the arguments for celibacy break down when that specter of loneliness just below the surface begins nudging at my together world. And the world of loneliness—a starkly honest naked world—comes up to meet me, and I sense the disarming presence of my God. Nothing tangible. But there. "Be still and know that I am God." Sometimes I want to run screaming the other way. I often wonder, if I had not taken this road, whether I would have ever come to face this realm of loneliness as I have.

Celibacy makes sense only if God is real, and trying to defend it in the market-place is like chasing gossamers on an autumn day. Like Harry who decided to be a priest five years after he was ordained, I sense that I am only slowly beginning to understand what I chose on my ordination day.

From time to time I come across my box of mementos as a teacher—eight years of them—and that red and white button "CHASTE MAKES WASTE" rolls up in the rubble. I smile affectionately at the memories of those high school kids. And in my more mundane moments I still do wonder about the rhyme of it all.

Winter thoughts. Nothing wrong with winter. It's a time of effort, of absorbing work and reflection—not for festivals and lemonade in the shade. Winter is for serious stuff. For some of us celibates it is a winter priesthood, and one we do observe without regret each December 21—close to the hearth.

A Married Layman
on Celibacy

JOHN GARVEY

FOR YEARS CELIBATE CATHOLIC PRIESTS have spoken to Catholic married people about marriage. Some of what they have had to say is valuable, even at times helpful in a practical way. When their advice rings false, it is frequently discounted by married people on the grounds that the speaker, not having experienced marriage, couldn't really be expected to be authoritative. (This has been especially true in the area of sex. Couples whose marriages are at all happy know that sexual intercourse is a good deal more than a reproductive necessity, and in a happy marriage it is never primarily that; it is similarly not just a remedy for concupiscence. In fact, nothing seems to remedy concupiscence. If anyone has a cure short of Origen's, it would be kind to let the rest of us know.)

In a similar spirit, I would like to offer this reflection on celibacy. I have observed priests, monks and nuns from childhood on, and know many quite well. Just as priests have offered the argument that an impartial observer of marriage can sometimes be a more qualified commentator than someone intimately involved, so perhaps a married layman might have something of value to say; and I invite the celibate reader to discount whatever seems unauthoritative or not quite to the point.

It has been pointed out that celibacy is under attack from the culture at large, and the discussion of a married clergy has in some cases been confused with a call to abolish celibacy altogether. I should make it clear at the outset that I regard celibacy as an important thing; where it is genuine, it is a gift to the Church. I am not concerned here with celibacy as a *sine qua non* for the priesthood, but with the vow itself.

And this is where we must begin, because there is something essential in the fact that celibacy is a *vowed* state, not simply a condition like being single by choice or by accident; and in this it is like marriage. This is important, because vows, in or out of marriage, are increasingly regarded as less than central. I don't mean to suggest that those who seek a dispensation from vows—those of the professed celibate religious or those of marriage—are to be condemned for doing so; but it should be clear that what they are being dispensed from is ideally a binding and (to use an unfashionable word) absolute thing. The Latin roots of the word *vow* are also found in the words *devoted* and *devotion.* The devoted person is the person of the vow. There may be perfectly good reasons for which an individual would look for a dispensation from a vow; but the possibility of dispensation should not make a vow seem at the start to be optional, something to be backed away from when things don't come up to expectations. Half-devotion is a contradiction in terms. There must be a whole-heartedness about undertaking the vowed life in any state; and it is a whole-heartedness which will simply have to be willed at times, especially in those dark times when there is no apparent reason to go on.

Western culture in recent years has tended to regard the idea of the vow as an anachronism based upon unreasonable expectations. A culture which is increasingly geared toward self-fulfillment and present satisfaction is not likely to be very sensitive in the way it looks at any vow. Vowing is, in a way, always done in the dark. It is an act of faith and hope: faith that what the vow entails is possible, and hope that the resources to make it possible will be there. There is something profoundly unreasonable about a vow—unreasonable here meaning beyond reason, not irrational. Any healthy young man or woman who takes a vow of celibacy, believing that he or she knows everything that the vow will involve, will be proved wrong. A couple who marry usually do not, at the time of their marriage, know one another very well. (They may think they do, but in retrospect they find out how wrong they were.) The young celibate, or the young husband or wife, knows enough about the life being undertaken to be willing to stake everything on the vow; but this is where the darkness begins, because we really do not know everything that will be asked of us.

The obvious question here is: Why do it at all? If there is an alternative to risking everything, why take the risk?

The answer, I think, is that without the vow we are much less likely to be led into the fullness of our humanity, which is a divine fullness. We will remain only human.

A vow is a symbol. Like all symbols, it has the power to evoke more than a merely rational, calculated response. To give your word before God that you will accept a vowed life, with anything it might involve, is an act of profound trust, which—if the vow is lived truly—draws you out of yourself, and draws from you responses and capabilities which you didn't know were there. To vow is to step into a larger life than the life you control and manipulate. Any part of the self which holds back poisons the vow, and makes living it that much more difficult. Vows are considered less than central to the business of being a human today because of the individualism which pervades Western culture: unless something can be shown to be of obvious and more or less immediate benefit to the individual, its value is questioned. The vow challenges this mentality by suggesting that self-fulfillment and personal freedom, good as they are, are not only not enough to make for a good life; a life which sets them as goals is too small a life. As Christians we are called to something larger and stranger than the life the world offers us; we are called to a deeper life, which discloses itself during the course of our life and is fulfilled at death. This, anyway, is our hope, the risk we take, and our evidence, such as it is, is to be found in the lives of people who went before us and lived well.

But if a vow, whether of marriage or of celibacy, calls us out of ourselves to a larger life—a participation in God's own life—what, specifically, does the vow of celibacy tell about that life? Marriage is easier to understand, certainly. The desires for companionship, love-making and children are universal and require no explanation. Within marriage there is the possibility of a knowing and a being known which is so archetypical of the soul's relationship to God that it is a recurrent theme in mystical literature (and of course, just as in the life of prayer, the knowing and being known involved in marriage can be humiliating and uncomfortable). Paul compares the love of one spouse for another to the love of Christ for the Church. In marriage the natural and the supernatural meet wonderfully.

But celibacy? That's the strange one. There is not

much in the Judaism from which Christianity sprang to make room for it. The monastic Essene community included celibates; but this was never common or encouraged in Judaism. The religions outside of Christianity which maintain celibate traditions tend either to deny or to undervalue the goodness of the world. Yet in our tradition, which says firmly that the world is good, that sex and procreation are good, that pleasure well-taken is loved by God, there is this bunch of men and women who do not marry, who are pledged to a life of abstinence from sex.

There is nothing obviously good or healthy about celibacy. That alone should be looked at, because we live in an in-between time. We are close enough to a Christian culture, in which celibacy was generally accepted, to be blinded to its strangeness, and at the same time we are distant from any common understanding which could allow celibacy to be seen as the shocking and necessary thing it is. The development of this understanding matters as much as anything else, if we are to see celibacy clearly. Consider this: celibacy seen as *desirable* would be neurotic, or selfish, or both. A person who refrains from marriage because he or she is afraid of the intimacy involved in marriage, or can't be bothered with it, or who does not want to be troubled by the burden of another person, or who does not want to be saddled with children, has made an ungenerous choice, a choice to be less than fully human. This is not at all what celibacy should be like.

Jesus says that celibacy is undertaken for the sake of the Kingdom of heaven by those whose hearts can bear it; it is not demanded of all his followers, as some Gnostics claimed. How does celibacy serve the Kingdom? If, as Jewish and Christian tradition insists, creation is good, what is good or holy about renouncing the goodness of marriage and parenthood? The radical nature of celibacy demands the renunciation of something wholly good—a fact which presents us with a paradox.

Most explanations of celibacy try, one way or another, to resolve this paradox. There is, for example, the argument that the celibate is more available, more able to give himself to those in need, because he is not tied down to wife and child; in this way he is devoted wholly to the Kingdom in a way that married people cannot be.

I don't find this convincing. For one thing, I have yet to meet a celibate whose celibacy had directly to do with his availability. By this I do not mean that I haven't met genuinely generous celibates—I have. But they were not *more* generous than the generous doctors I have known, or the generous married couples whose homes have been havens for many people, whose lives are open to those in need at every moment. And while there are kinds of work in which celibacy is, in a practical sense, more convenient (for example, the constant work of Mother Teresa with Calcutta's dying, or the work of many others with the poor), even this kind of work has at times been done selflessly by married couples. An argument from practicality, it seems to me, sells celibacy short.

Another argument is that the celibate, in committing his love to no particular person, is free to love everyone. But this contradicts the experience of love by making it a rationed thing, as if having spent seventy-five litres of love on one's wife and children, one had only twenty-five litres of God's allotment left for the rest of the race. In fact, by learning to love one other person deeply, one learns to love every other person that much more deeply. The love that a man and woman have for one another and for their children is, if it is Christian, carried into the rest of their lives and into every other relationship. Unless a person is capable of loving one other person deeply—and this is as true of celibates as it is of married people—he is not capable of loving *anyone,* much less everyone. There is nothing at all abstract about love; the incarnation should teach us that much. And John reminds us that if we cannot love the one we see before us, we cannot love God, who cannot be seen.

Still another and more recent argument is that the celibate combines in himself both male and female elements, exhibiting a wholeness which others must seek in the opposite sex. But this also falls short of experience. In a good marriage, a man and woman learn from one another's differences. "Masculine" and "feminine" attributes (which are increasingly seen as stereotypical, when they are gendered that way) must come together in any mature individual, celibate or married.

The paradoxical nature of celibacy should not be explained away or made to look like a practical and beneficial thing. I believe it was Cardinal Suhard who said that as Christians we should live in such a way that, if God did not exist, our lives would make no sense. I am sure he did not mean that we are meant to put on a sort of show for the sake of the world, but rather meant to point out the risk of true Christianity: finally, you have to put everything on the line. It is unfortunate that asceticism has come to have such a bad name in recent years; perhaps this bad name is the inevitable reaction to the misrepresentation of asceticism to which many of us were exposed, which made it seem a simple hatred of the flesh. It is unfortunate, because only within the context of a refreshed sense of the ascetic can celibacy make sense.

Celibacy is a kind of fast. Like fasting from food and drink, like voluntary poverty, it makes no worldly sense. It makes sense only if God is real. Like fasting and voluntary poverty, celibacy is a witness to a life which is more profoundly *real* than the life offered by the world. Celibacy has no worldly justification (and this is why practical, sensible arguments in its favor sell it short, just as the argument that fasting is good for the figure misses the point of fasting), but it makes sense in the context of the reality of God's Kingdom. Like fasting, it involves a focus that there are priorities which demand radical responses. Like voluntary poverty, it may have to be a lifelong thing to bear the fruit it is meant to bear.

How are any of these things helpful? Fasting, like celibacy, means refraining from something good. It is a way of affirming that God alone is enough, is in fact everything, and it helps focus our attention on God. During a fast we are reminded continuously (and sometimes uncomfortably) of what our lives are really about. The person who lives in radical simplicity, giving away what he does not need, has in a similar way put his life on the line.

Celibacy is in the same way a witness to the wholeheartedness the Gospel demands. This singleness must be present in every Christian life, not just the life of the celibate; but celibacy helps to illuminate it, to throw it into relief. It is easy to say, for example, that I am ready to drop everything for the sake of the Kingdom, that once my hand is on the plow I will not turn back. It is willingness that matters, of course; but never to see that willingness tested can lead us into self-deception, which is a lesson fasting can teach us. At the level of the community, celibacy offers the same sort of witness to the married Christian. It is a manifestation of the fact that there is a love which suffices absolutely, and it is offered to each single human being, as well as to the community.

This love is what celibacy reveals, or should reveal. It is obviously not an easy witness to bear, as Jesus himself said, and it is certainly not for everyone. It is a negative thing, in that it means self-denial, and at times whatever good it may offer will be invisible to the person who endures the loneliness which is an inevitable part of celibacy, for anyone with enough heart to love. The person who fasts from food will be hungry, and the person who fasts from sex, and the long intimate companionship of marriage, and from parenthood, will experience intense loneliness. Just as marriage and parenthood have their dark moments (there is no distance so lonely as the distance which can occur between two people who love one another, and a child's serious illness involves parents in an agony with which others may sympathize, but which can be shared only by someone who has gone through the same agony) so celibacy has a depth of loneliness which must be acknowledged, not to get it out of the way—that can't be done—but to bring it to healing, by allowing the community to share as much of the burden as can be shared, and by asking the community to be available during the darkest moments.

Here it is important to realize that one danger of celibacy is the myth of self-sufficiency. The celibates I know who live it well are, not at all coincidentally, the ones who are capable of forming deep friendships, and who never give the sense of having erected protective emotional barriers. Many of them are members of religious orders, who come from communities human enough to provide their members with the mutual support and companionship which all of us must receive from our families and friends. I point this out because of the chilling barrenness too often encountered in rectories and convents, and in individual celibates whose inability to deal with the simplest heartfelt emotion is pitiful. A sour celibacy is at least as scandalous and hurtful to the community as a bad marriage.

In the Eastern churches it has been the typical practice to ordain married men, leaving celibacy to monks, from whom the bishops are chosen. This ancient discipline points up two things which the Western Church may have forgotten. One is that celibacy, like the monastic life, is a radical choice. The other is that it must be situated in an ascetic, contemplative context. Celibacy without asceticism and prayerfulness could become the most refined, subtle selfishness in the world. Perhaps Catholicism in the past did overemphasize the cross, suffering, and self-denial. But excluding these Christian facts is not the remedy; it is rather a surrender to the cultural surroundings that will only allow the sort of religion that fits in, the religion which reinforces the picture the world wants to have of itself. C. S. Lewis once remarked that there is always a tendency to warn an age against the danger into which it is least likely to fall; so in a puritanical age we are warned against licentiousness, and in a licentious age we are warned against puritanism. It isn't the dangers of asceticism that the Western world needs to fear right now.

There is one final, pastoral aspect of celibacy which I would like to mention. There are people who remain unmarried and unloved because they have not been able, for whatever reasons, to attract anyone. In looking at a married person someone in this situation is able to say, "He couldn't possibly understand my loneliness—he lives in such security, the security of being loved." The fact that the other person is loved stands as a barrier between them. The celibate can reveal to someone this lonely a love which can be healing, and can restore a meaning and dignity which the world denies.

Celibacy seen only as a "state in life" is as cold as ice, just as dead as a marriage which exists only as a pledge on paper. It must exhibit the love it is based in, the paradoxical strength and weakness of which Paul boasts, or it will be worthless.

Sex, God and the Church

SEBASTIAN MOORE, O.S.B.

IT IS SURELY NECESSARY, at this time of rapid cultural shift, to attempt to get a wide-angle view of sexual morals and of the Church's presence in this sphere. So I want to share with you some thinking I have been doing recently, whose purpose has been to discover the connection, in experience, between sexuality and God. For the sake of clarity, we need to attempt some formulation of the fundamental problem of human sexuality. This may seem an oversimplifying approach, but perhaps it is worth attempting. I spoke of a wide-angle view, after all.

I have found, first, that a crucial concept is that of sexual identity. I accept as broadly true the Freudian belief that the main foundations of the person-to-be are laid by about age five. By then, the whole package is put together in a rudimentary way. We have already characterized the stages of this assembling as follows. From zero to one-plus, I was "will." From then to three-four, I was the beginning of a "person." Finally, around four-five, I was "boy" or "girl." My sexual identity is the final and the fullest edition or version of myself, of what I am to think of myself as.

Sexual identity, once it emerges, is heavily endorsed by the culture's idea of what men and women are like. But it seems to me vital to be clear that the effect of the culture, though powerful and fateful, is to *interpret* the sexual difference, not to *create* it.

I have long wondered why sexual identity is so important and has always been thought to be so. The best reason I can come up with is that for all the scope of his or her mind, the human being is not independent but is woven into a whole continuum of nature. The points of contact for this interweave are dependence on the earth for sustenance, sexuality, and mortality. These provide, according to Northrop Frye, the only three universal human images: of food as sacred, of mating as sacred, and of life as a journey. They also provide, universally, the three themes of the so-called "shadow language"—words that are only written on walls. Sustenance, sex and death are the three great reminders of our incompleteness, our fragility. But whereas need and death press indifferently on all persons, sex makes a difference between two sorts of persons. It makes a deeper inroad into personhood. It gets right into personhood, to name the person as one or the other half of the human whole. The reminder that men and women get of their incompleteness by looking at their body sexually is a subtler, deeper, and above all more emotionally involving reminder than that of the pangs of hunger and mortality.

Another thing has to be said, however, about the three reminders. They not only remind. They accentuate what I call a cosmic loneliness. For the self-aware being, alone in the cosmos, asks who he/she is. Self-awareness seeks a place to be, seeks to *have* a place, to belong, seeks for his/her meaning. And when, impelled thus to question, I ask *nature* who I am, nature is silent. This silence brings home to me that, at root, I am lonely. The human being, says Loren Eiseley, is the cosmic orphan.

Now let's put these two ideas together: that the three experiences of our interweaving with nature awaken in us a cosmic loneliness; and that, *of* these three experiences, the sexual makes the deepest inroad of nature into our *identity*. It follows from this conjunction that my sexual identity gives me an especially strong sense of cosmic loneliness.

The importance of this phenomenon is that my maleness looks not only to woman and to mating but to whatever it is that may speak to me where nature is silent. In other words, people are sexually involved with the lonely problem of God and meaning, and not only with each other contrasexually. The enormous cultural investment, in all cultures, in the assigning and endorsing of sex *roles,* is evidence of this powerful preoccupation in people with making sense of themselves *as* men, *as* women, quite apart from their complementarity in union. Popular psychology has given us all sorts of ideas of the different factors involved in sexual intimacy—such as "that there are always at least four people in the bed"—but the most important thing to consider is that each of the parties is looking in two opposite directions: to the other, and within the self.

The "two looks" are not at all easy to align. In fact, if we are to attempt a single answer to our opening question "What *is* the sexual problem?" it is here: How do we align passion with friendship? How do we align sex as powerful attraction to another with sex as "who I am," with sex as that "final edition of personhood"?

My belief is that they are out of alignment *because* we are "cosmic orphans." Sexuality makes us lonely as well as drawing us to each other. This idea is simply and poignantly expressed in the story of the Fall, which might have been called "How Cosmic Loneliness Began": "She ate of the fruit and gave some to her husband and he ate. And immediately their eyes were opened, and they saw that they were naked. So they sewed for themselves loincloths out of figleaves." The *immediate* effect of losing touch with God is the awkwardness of the sexes with each other, through the involvedness of *each* with his/her loneliness, with the lost God. And this awkwardness, this nonalignment, is the root of all our sexual disorders. The Christian tradition has been so much preoccupied *with* these disorders that it has seen *them* as the immediate consequence of the Fall. It has failed so far to understand that being out of touch with God means being *out of friendship* with my body and its desires, rather than being *no longer master* of my desires. Shame generates lust, not lust shame.

Now we must look at history. For if our cosmic loneliness entails an immense preoccupation of each sex with itself, our culture since the dawn of civilization has overwhelmingly emphasized the male quest for identity over the female. The male "ideal-types"—of warrior, knight, monk, sage, king, priest—heavily predominate. If woman figures at all in the quest for identity, she is the seductress, the temptress, the witch, the siren who lures man off course and onto the rocks—man in search of his identity, his Holy Grail. This is the shape of the patriarchal age, which, according to some scholars, was originally a breakaway from a matriarchal age in which the "non-alignment" was hardly felt because self-awareness was hardly present.

Now that gives us two *more* ideas to put together: the non-alignment of sexual identity with sexual attraction, and the heavy cultural endorsement of male sexual identity over against female. This means that men, *alienated* from women through cosmic loneliness, and seeing them-

selves as the more *emphasized* sex, interpret their alienation as a challenge to *dominate* women. The primordial
alienation goes into the cultural mold of the master-slave
paradigm. *Control* is the name of the game. And if we ask
how the theologian interpreters of the Genesis text
achieved the unanimous corporate oversight of seeing *loss
of control* as the primary consequence of the Fall where the
text is saying that *awkwardness between the sexes* is the primary consequence, we surely have our answer: the text is
being read with the eyes of the patriarchal mentality, for
which man is the center, woman the hazard, and control
the name of the game.

Now the game is up, the patriarchal age is everywhere in crisis and indeed threatening us with extinction,
and there is beginning the woman's quest for *her* identity,
a quest of comparable magnitude with the male quest that
has shaped three millennia. German philosopher Karl Jaspers saw an "axial shift" occurring around the sixth century B.C.—coincident with the tragedy of Oedipus Rex and
the birth of the patriarchal age—and he described the
present age as a second axial shift. He said, "During this
century it has been slowly dawning on us that scores of
centuries are coming to a close."

And in the middle of all this, we have the Catholic
Church, which, institutionally, is the most patriarchal body
there is. Its *idea* of sexuality, shaped by generations of
male celibates and prescribed by a male celibate magisterium, is very much that of the patriarchal age, its implict
theme, "Men, control yourselves (and control the women
too)." Hence, I am sure, its failure to touch people today,
even people of the best will in the world.

But I must leave you with a paradox. This same
Church owes its existence and its meaning to an experience two thousand years ago, in which a small body of

women and men knew the ending of cosmic loneliness, the liberation of the human psyche in Christ from all its barriers internal and external. If there is any community in the world that *ought* to understand that people don't like sex because they don't know God, that community is the Catholic Church. And that the patriarchal model *is* breaking down in the Church is suggested by the way a priest— Andrew Greeley—can say in a principal Catholic weekly that the pronouncements of the recent Roman synod came from celibate men and evidence their dislike of sex and of women.

So there's my wide-angle vision, splayed out in all its paradoxical unmanageableness! The Church *is* committed to a strict and exacting sexual ethic, the reason for which is the high price that must be paid for sexual fulfillment. But people don't believe that that *is* the Church's reason. And, by and large, they are right!

Celibacy and the Holy

HENRI J. M. NOUWEN

INTRODUCTION

WHEN YOU LOOK OUT over the city of Rome, walk in its streets, or ride in its buses, you quickly realize that it is a crowded city full of houses, full of people, full of cars, yes—even full of cats. You see men and women moving quickly in all directions, you hear joyful and angry voices mixed with a great variety of street sounds, you smell many odors—especially cappuccino—and you feel the Italian embrace by which you gain a friend or lose your money. It is a busy, congested city, in which life manifests itself in all its boisterous intensity.

But in the midst of this lively and colorful conglomeration of houses, people, and cars, there are the domes of Rome pointing to the places set apart for the Holy One. The churches of Rome are like beautiful frames around empty spaces witnessing to him who is the quiet, still center of all human life. The churches are not useful, not practical, not requiring immediate action or quick response. They are spaces without loud noises, hungry movements, or impatient gestures. They are tranquil

158

spaces, strangely empty most of the time. They speak a language different from the world around them. They do not want to be museums. They want to invite us to be silent, to sit or kneel, to listen attentively, and to rest with our whole being.

A city without carefully protected empty spaces where one can sense the silence from which all words grow, and rest in the stillness from which all actions flow, such a city is in danger of losing its real center.

I wonder if the busy city with its many quiet places cannot offer us an image of what celibacy might mean in our contemporary society. After all, isn't the active street life that part of us that wants to be with others, to move and to produce, and isn't the dome carefully protecting some empty space, that other part of us that needs to be protected and even defended to prevent our lives from losing their center? Our inner sanctum, that inner, holy place, that sacred center in our lives where only God may enter, that is as important for our lives as the domes are for the city of Rome. Much can be said about celibacy. But I want to reflect on it from just one perspective. I want to look at celibacy as a witness to the inner sanctum in our own lives and in the lives of others. By giving a special visibility to this inner sanctum, this holy, empty space in human life, the celibate man or woman wants to affirm and proclaim that all human intimacy finds its deepest meaning and fulfillment when it is experienced and lived as a participation in the intimacy of God himself.

In order to explore the meaning of the witness of the celibate life, I would like to focus on three areas: first on the world in which celibacy is lived; then on the nature of the witness that the celibate offers to this world; and finally on the life-style by which this witness is enhanced and strengthened.

THE WORLD

The Limits of the Interpersonal

The world in which celibacy wants to be a witness for a holy, empty space is a world that puts great emphasis on interpersonal relationships. We can safely say that in the Western culture of the last few decades the value of coming together, being together, living together, and loving together has received more attention than ever before. The healing power of eye contact, of attentive listening, and of the careful touch has been explored by many psychologists, sensitivity trainers, and communication experts. Practically every year you can hear about a new type of therapy, a new form of consciousness enlarging, or a new method of communication. Many, many people suffering from feelings of isolation, alienation, or loneliness have found new hope and strength in these experiments in togetherness. Just seeing the great popularity and the growing influence of re-evaluation therapy is enough to convince a sympathetic observer that a deep need is being responded to.

We indeed need each other and are able to give each other much more than we often realize. Too long have we been burdened by fear and guilt, and too long have we denied each other the affection and closeness we rightly desire. We, therefore, have much to learn from those who are trying to open up new and more creative interpersonal relations.

But critical questions still need to be raised. Can real intimacy be reached without a deep respect for that holy place within and between us, that space that should remain untouched by human hands? Can human intimacy really be fulfilling when every space within and between us is being filled up? Is the emphasis on the healing possibilities of human togetherness not often the result of a one-sided perception of our human predicament? These questions have a new urgency in the time of the human-potential movements. I often wonder if we do not think or feel that our painful experiences of loneliness are primarily results of a lack of interpersonal closeness. We seem to think: "If I could just break through my fear to express my real feelings of love and hostility, if I could just feel free to hold a friend, if I could just talk honestly and openly with my own people, if I could just live with someone who really cares . . . then I would have again some inner peace and experience again some inner wholeness." When any of these experiences have become reality to us we feel, in fact, a certain relief, but the question remains if it is there that the real source of our healing and wholeness can be found. In a world in which traditional patterns of human communications have broken down and in which family, profession, and village no longer offer the intimate bonds they did in the past, the basic human condition of aloneness has entered so deeply into our emotional awareness that we are constantly tempted to want more from our fellow human beings than they can give. If we relate to our neighbors with the supposition that they are able to fulfill our deepest needs, we will find ourselves increasingly frustrated, because, when we expect a friend or lover to be able to take away our deepest pain, we expect from him or her something that cannot be given by human beings. No human being can understand us fully, no human being can give us unconditional love, no human being can offer constant affection, no human being can enter into the core of our being and heal our deepest brokenness. When we forget that and expect from others more than they can give, we will be quickly disillusioned; for when we do not receive what we expect, we easily become resentful, bitter, revengeful, and even violent.

Lately we have become very much aware of the fragile border between intimacy and violence. We see or hear about cruelty between husband and wife, parents and children, brothers and sisters, and start realizing that those who desire so desperately to be loved find themselves often entangled in violent relationships. The stories in the daily paper about sexual aggression, mutilation, and murder evoke the vision of people desperately grasping each other and clinging to each other, crying out and shouting for love, but not receiving anything but more violence.

Spinoza's words "Nature abhors a vacuum" seem quite applicable to us, and the temptation is indeed very great to take flight into an intimacy and closeness that does not leave any open space. Much suffering results from this suffocating closeness.

With Praying Hands

I found a good image to describe our predicament in the book *Existential Metapsychiatry* by New York psychiatrist Thomas Hora (New York: Seabury Press, 1977, p. 32). Thomas Hora calls the great emphasis on interpersonal relationships as the way to healing *personalism,* and he compares this personalism with the interlocking fingers of two hands. The fingers of the two hands can intertwine only to the point that a stalemate is reached. After that the only possible movement is backward, causing friction and eventually pain. And too much friction leads to separation. When we relate to each other as the interlocking fingers of two hands we enter into a suffocating closeness that does not leave any free space. When lonely people with a strong desire for intimacy move closer and closer to each other in the hope of coming to an experience of belonging and wholeness, all too frequently they find themselves locked in a situation in which closeness leads to friction, friction to pain, and pain to separation.

Many marriages are so short-lived precisely because there is an intense desire for closeness and a miminimal amount of space that allows for free movement. Because of the high emotional expectation with which they enter into a relationship, married couples often panic when they do not experience the inner contentment for which they had hoped. Often they try very hard to alleviate their tensions by exploring in much detail their life together, only to end up in a stalemate, tired, exhausted, and finally forced to separate in order to avoid mutual harm.

Thomas Hora suggests as the image for a true human relationship two hands coming together parallel in a prayerful gesture, pointing beyond themselves and moving freely in relation to one another. I find this a helpful image exactly because it makes it clear that a mature human intimacy requires a deep and profound respect for the free and empty space that needs to exist within and between partners and that asks for a continuous mutual protection and nurture. Only in this way can a relationship be lasting, precisely because mutual love is experienced as a participation in a greater and earlier love to which it points. In this way intimacy can be rich and fruitful, since it has been given carefully protected space in which to grow. This relationship no longer is a fearful clinging to each other but a free dance, allowing space in which we can move forward and backward, form constantly new patterns, and see each other as always new.

The world in which we live is a world with many fearful, lonely, and anxious people clinging to each other to find some relief, some satisfaction, and some joy. The

tragedy of our world is that much of the intense desire for
love, acceptance, and belonging is cruelly turned into jealousy, resentment, and violence, often to the bitter surprise
of those who had no other desire than to live in peace and
love.

In this world with many people anxiously clinging to
each other, a sign of hope needs to be given. In this world
celibacy, as a visible manifestation of the holy space in an
overcrowded world, can be a powerful witness in service
of mature human relationships.

THE WITNESS

Vacancy for God

The best definition of celibacy, I think, is the definition of Thomas Aquinas. Thomas calls celibacy a vacancy
for God. To be a celibate means to be empty for God, to
be free and open for his presence, to be available for his
service. This view on celibacy, however, has often led to
the false idea that being empty for God is a special privi-
lege of celibates, while other people involved in all sorts
of interpersonal relationship are not empty but full, occu-
pied as well as preoccupied. If we look at celibacy as a
state of life that upholds the importance of God's presence
in our lives in contrast with other states of life that lead to
entanglement in worldly affairs, we quickly slip into a dangerous elitism considering celibates as domes rising up
amid the many low houses of the city.

I think that celibacy can never be considered as a special prerogative of a few members of the people of God.
Celibacy, in its deepest sense of creating and protecting
emptiness for God, is an essential part of all forms of

Christian life: marriage, friendship, single life, and community life. We will never fully understand what it means to be celibate unless we recognize that celibacy is, first of all, an element, and even an essential element in the life of all Christians. Let me illustrate how this is true in marriage and friendship.

Marriage is not a lifelong attraction of two individuals to each other, but a call for two people to witness together to God's love. The basis of marriage is not mutual affection, or feelings, or emotions and passions that we associate with love, but a vocation, a being elected to build together a house for God in this world, to be like the two cherubs whose outstretched wings sheltered the ark of the covenant and created a space where Yahweh could be present (Ex 25:10–12; 1 Kgs 8:6–7). Marriage is a relationship in which a man and a woman protect and nurture the inner sanctum within and between them and witness to that by the way in which they love each other. Marriage, too, is therefore a *vacare Deo.* Celibacy is part of marriage not simply because married couples may have to be able to live separated from each other for long periods of time, because they may need to abstain from sexual relations for physical, mental, or spiritual reasons, but also because the intimacy of marriage itself is an intimacy that is based on the common participation in a love greater than the love two people can offer each other. The real mystery of marriage is not that husband and wife love each other so much that they can find God in each other's lives, but that God loves them so much that they can discover each other more and more as living reminders of his divine presence. They are brought together, indeed, as two prayerful hands extended toward God and forming in this way a home for him in this world.

The same thing is true for friendship. Deep and ma-

ture friendship does not mean that we keep looking each
other in the eyes and are constantly impressed or enrap-
tured by each other's beauty, talents, and gifts, but it
means that together we look at him who calls us to his service.

I was deeply impressed by the way the members of
the San Egidio community in Trastevere described their
relationship with each other. They made it very clear to
me that friendship is very important to them, but that they
have to learn in their apostolate to keep seeing their relationships with each other in the context of their common
call. As soon as the relationship itself becomes central they
are moving away from their vocation. They have to be
willing to let new developments in their apostolate separate them from each other for certain periods of time, and
they also have to be willing to see and experience their
separations as an invitation to deepen their relationship
with their Lord and through him with each other. That is
why they feel so strongly that their weekly Eucharist and
their daily vespers form the source of their love for each
other. There they find each other as friends, there they
strengthen their commitment to each other, and there
they find the courage to follow their Lord even when he
asks them to go in different directions. Thus their relationship is really a standing together around the altar or
around the holy empty space indicated by the icon. Together they want to protect the empty space in and between each other.

Thus marriage and friendship carry within their center a holy vacancy, a space that is for God and God alone.
Without that holy center, marriage as well as friendship
becomes like a city without domes, a city forgetting the
meaning and direction of its own activities.

Living Reminders

We can now see that celibacy has a very important place in our world. The celibate makes his life into a visible witness for the priority of God in our lives, a sign to remind all people that without the inner sanctum our lives lose contact with their source and goal. We belong to God. All people do. Celibates are people who, by not attaching themselves to any one particular person, remind us that the relationship with God is the beginning, the source, and the goal of all human relationships.

By his or her life of non-attachment, the celibate lifts up an aspect of the Christian life of which we all need to be reminded. The celibate is like the clown in the circus who, between the scary acts of the trapeze artists and lion tamers, fumbles and falls, reminding us that all human activities are ultimately not so important as the virtuosi make us believe. Celibates live out the holy emptiness in their lives by not marrying, by not trying to build for themselves a house or a fortune, by not trying to wield as much influence as possible, and by not filling their lives with events, people, or creations for which they will be remembered. They hope that by their empty lives God will be recognized as the source of all human thoughts and actions. Especially by not marrying and by abstaining from the most intimate expression of human love, the celibate becomes a living sign of the limits of interpersonal relationships and of the centrality of the inner sanctum that no human being may violate.

To whom, then, is this witness directed? I dare to say that celibacy is, first of all, a witness to all those who are married. I wonder if we have explored enough the very important relationship between marriage and celibacy.

Lately we have become aware of this interrelatedness in a very painful way. The crisis of celibacy and the crisis of married life appeared together. At the same time that many priests and religious persons move away from the celibate life, we see many couples questioning the value of their commitment to each other. These two phenomena, although they are not connected with each other as cause and effect, are closely related because marriage and celibacy are two ways of living within the Christian community that support each other. Celibacy is a support to married people in their commitment to each other. The celibate reminds those who live together in marriage of their own celibate center, which they need to protect and nurture in order to live a life that does not depend simply upon the stability of emotions and affections, but also on their common love for God, who called them together. On the other hand, married people also witness to those who have chosen the celibate life, reminding them that it is the love of God that indeed makes rich and creative human relationships possible and that the value of the celibate life becomes manifest in a generous, affectionate, and faithful care for those in need. Married people remind celibates that celibates also live in covenant and are brides and grooms. Thus celibacy and marriage need each other.

Celibates can indeed have a very good understanding of married life and married people of celibate life. Remarks such as "You don't know what you are talking about because you are not married (or celibate)" can be very misleading. Precisely because marriage and celibacy are in each other's service and bound together by their common witness to God's love as the love from which all human relationships originate, celibate and married people can be of invaluable help to each other by supporting their different life-styles.

Celibacy not only witnesses to the inner sanctum to married people, but also, together with marriage, celibacy speaks of the presence of God in the world to anyone who is there to listen. In a world so congested and so entangled in conflict and pain, celibates by their dedication to God in a single life-style, and married people by their dedication to God in a life together, are signs of God's presence in this world. They both ask us in different ways to turn to God as the source of all human relationships. They both say in different ways that without giving God his rightful place in the midst of the city, we all die in the hopeless attempt to fabricate peace and love by ourselves. The celibate speaks of the need to respect the inner sanctum at all cost; the married Christian speaks of the need to base human relationships on the intimacy with God himself. But both speak for God and his Lordship in the world, and together they give form to the Christian community and stand out as signs of hope.

Thus, in a world torn by loneliness and conflict and trying so hard to create better human relationships, celibacy is a very important witness. It encourages us to create space for him who sent his Son, thus revealing to us that we can only love each other because he has loved us first.

THE LIFE-STYLE

Useless . . .

When we look at celibacy as a *vacare Deo,* a being empty for God as a visible witness for the inner sanctum in all people's lives, then it becomes clear that sexual abstinence can never be the most important aspect of celibacy. Not being married or not being involved in a sexual relationship does not constitute the celibate life. Celibacy is an openness to God of which sexual abstinence is only one of its manifestations. Celibacy is a life-style in which we try to witness to the priority of God in all relationships. This involves every part of our life, the way we eat and drink, work and play, sleep and rest, speak and be silent. It is an openness to God acted out in such a way that it must raise questions in those we encounter. It is a sort of lifelong street theater constantly trying to raise questions in people's minds about the deeper meaning of their own existence.

Therefore we need to see celibacy as a life-style in which we witness to God's place in this world in many ways other than sexual abstinence. I would like to discuss two aspects of celibacy that today are of special importance for a life-style that emphasizes life as a vacancy for God. They are contemplative prayer and voluntary poverty.

Contemplative prayer is an essential element of the celibate life, because it is first of all an attitude of being empty for God. Contemplative prayer is not a way of being busy with God instead of with people, but it is an attitude in which we recognize God's ultimate priority by being useless in his presence, by standing in front of him without anything to show, to prove, or to argue, and by allowing him to enter into our emptiness. Thus, an intimate connection exists between celibacy and contemplative prayer. Both are expressions of being vacant for God. In our utilitarian culture, in which we suffer from a collective compulsion to do something practical, helpful, or useful, and to make a contribution that can give us a sense of worth, contemplative prayer is a form of radical criticism. It is not useful or practical but a way of wasting time for God. It cuts a hole in our busyness and reminds us and others that it is God and not we who creates and sustains the world. Contemplative prayer as standing naked, powerless, and vulnerable before God, therefore, is one of the most important expressions of the celibate life-style.

In this useless prayer, God can show us his love. When we are empty, free, and open, we can be with him, look at him, listen to him, and slowly begin to realize that he is our loving Father who loves us with a deep, intimate affection. It is very important for a celibate to develop a very warm, affective, and intimate prayer life in which the gentle, caring love of God can be experienced and enjoyed. In this contemplative prayer we become really free, we sense that we are accepted, that we belong, that we are not totally alone but that we live in the embrace of him whose fatherhood includes motherly, brotherly, and sisterly love. Once we really know him in prayer, then we can live in this world without a need to cling to anyone for self-affirmation, and then we can let the abundance of God's love be the source of all our ministry.

And poor . . .

Besides contemplative prayer, the celibate life-style also asks for voluntary poverty. A wealthy celibate is like a fat sprinter. Anyone who is serious about his celibacy has to ask himself, "Am I poor?" If the answer is, "No, I am much better off than most people, I can buy more than my parishioners, eat and drink better than those to whom I minister," then we have not yet taken our celibacy seriously. Voluntary poverty is probably one of the most important signs of a celibate life-style. In fact, many married people do not take celibacy seriously because they contrast their daily struggle to pay the bills for food, house, and education with the carefree life of celibates and wonder who is really living out the witness to the Gospel. If there

is one aspect of contemporary ministry that needs emphasis today it is voluntary poverty. In a time in which we
have become so aware of the sins of capitalism and hear
daily about the millions who suffer from lack of food,
shelter, and the most basic care, you cannot consider yourself a witness for God's presence when your own life is
cluttered with material possessions, your belly overfull,
and your mind crowded with worries about what to do
with what you have. In our days voluntary poverty is probably the most necessary form of our vacancy for God. It is
the most convincing sign of our solidarity with the world
as we know it today, and the most powerful support for a
life of sexual abstinence. Wherever the Church is vital, it
is poor. It is true in Rome: look at the work of the Missionaries of Charity, and at the Little Sisters and Brothers.
It is true in Latin America: look at the new forms of ministry in Mexico, Paraguay, and Brazil. It is true, too, in the
United States: look at the *Catholic Worker* and the Sojourners Community.

Wherever the Church renews itself it embraces voluntary poverty as a spontaneous response to the situation
in this world, a response that expresses criticism of the
growing wealth of the few and solidarity with the growing
misery of the many.

What this poverty means concretely in the life of each
of us is hard to say because this needs to be discerned in
everyone's individual life. But I dare say that anyone who
practices contemplative prayer in a disciplined way will be
confronted sooner or later with Christ's words to the rich
young man. Because if one thing is sure it is that we are all
rich young men asking, "Teacher, what must I do to possess everlasting life?" It is not so clear yet that we are
ready to hear the answer.

Thus we can say that contemplative prayer and voluntary poverty are the two main pillars that support a celibate life.

CONCLUSION

Trying to summarize and conclude these thoughts on celibacy, I am painfully aware that many questions you probably have about celibacy have hardly been touched. I have not discussed how our sexual drives, desires, and needs can be creatively integrated into a celibate life-style. I have not talked about the important relationship between celibacy and community life, and I have not spoken about the value of celibacy for a concrete day-to-day ministry. I wanted very consciously to avoid emphasizing the usefulness of celibacy. By speaking about celibacy as a way of life that makes us more available to our fellow human beings, that encourages us to share our gifts with many people, and that makes us more able to move freely to different places where the human needs ask most urgently for pastoral response . . . by speaking of celibacy in such a way I might make it too useful and take away too quickly the foolishness of making oneself a eunuch for the Kingdom of heaven (see Mt 19:12). Jesus did not present celibacy as a very practical, useful, and effective life-style. By saying about celibacy, "Let anyone accept this who can," he makes it clear that celibacy is not the most acceptable, understandable, or obvious choice in one's life. Making celibacy useful, therefore, would be more a tribute to the spirit of American pragmatism than to the spirit of the Gospel. To protect and nurture vacancy for God in the midst of a world that wants to offer self-fulfillment can hardly be useful or practical. Standing empty-handed in the presence of God is not useful, divesting oneself of possessions is not practical, and living a life without an intimate companion and without children is certainly not very smart.

But, still, contemplative prayer, voluntary poverty, and sexual abstinence are three elements of a celibate lifestyle that together witness to the necessity of creating a vacancy where we can listen to God's voice and celebrate his presence in our midst. Only when we are willing to accept the uselessness, impracticality, and foolishness of this lifestyle may celibacy prove to be effective after all. But this type of effectiveness does not belong to the world. It belongs to the Kingdom of God. And this type of effectiveness can only be known when we have fully experienced the pain of our emptiness.

In the circus of life we indeed are the clowns. Let us train ourselves well so that those who watch us will smile and recognize that in the midst of our crowded city, we have to keep a place for him who loves his stubborn and hard-headed children with an infinite tenderness and care.

PART THREE

——————————

SOCIAL DIMENSIONS OF CELIBACY

Christian Practice
in the Personal Form

JOHN F. KAVANAUGH, S.J.

COMMUNITY:
RESPONSE TO CULTURAL ISOLATIONISM

A LIFE OF FAITH AND OF HOPE AND OF LOVE rises
in contradiction to the values of the Commodity Form* in
our culture. Faith, hope, and love are the three human
activities deemed most impossible by the cognitive and
behavioral standards of commodity consciousness. In
Catholic tradition, one believes that these three human
acts are "theological virtues"—the highest exercise of our
human personhood, wherein we participate in the very
life of God. Thus, not surprisingly, the anti-humanism of
our culture is at the same time a lived atheism.

Lived belief, the lived practice of these theological
virtues, must conflict with the received conditioning of
our social, political, and theoretical systems. It is this conflict, as well as the facts that we are intrinsically social be-

---

*Cf. distinctions and examples in the tables at the end of this arti-
cle.

ings, that we are intrinsically inter-subjective, and that the revelation of God is in and through a community or a people, which lead us to a recognition of our need for community. Our faith vision is received only in terms of our history and psycho-social development; if it is to be nurtured and purified and sustained, it will also have to be in terms of our historicity and sociality.

Traditional religious communities (which we will briefly discuss later in this article) have been, despite the lapses, enduring focuses of shared communitarian faith and witness aspiring to the revelation of Jesus Christ. But today there are a number of newer emphases upon Christian community life: from a growing sense of a priest-brotherhood found in *Jesu Caritas* communities, to the Focolare movement, to the Jean Vanier communities of the handicapped, to counter-cultural Christian communities modeled after the Catholic Worker. The Cursillo movement and Christian Life Communities continue to develop, with regularly shared prayer and faith sessions, ongoing communication, and longer-range commitments. The Charismatic Renewal movement also emphasizes the communal dimension of praying, of healing (memories, physical and psychological suffering) in the context of community, of greater emphasis upon continuing personal contact and support within chosen or parish-located groups. The Marriage Encounter movement likewise stresses the communal sharing of faith, prayer, and some goods, and the mutual support of families in their commitment. The Sojourners, the New Jerusalem, and peace communities of activists all offer witness to faith, and service to men and women. Inner-city pastoral and justice groups undertake regular communal prayer and meetings of shared faith. Groups of informally gathered married couples study and discuss their vocations. Christian professional groups cluster in families for the confirming of life, ideals, hope, and plans. These are all examples of the movement among Christian people for a new sense of corporateness and communality.

All of these groupings are based on the discovery that a Christian, in the face of our culture's dwarfing and isolating of the individual, must turn to a community of shared life-experience which both fosters committed faith and enables the individual to criticize and challenge the programming of the culture. The most effective means by which both goals are achieved is in a communally shared Christian life.

Physical growth, both individual and social, is cellular; the same principle applies to the life of faith. Christian cell-communities should be formed which will call forth (a) an internal fidelity of the members to a life of prayer, shared faith, and mutual encouragement and correction, (b) an internal critique of personal and community actions, apostolates, and goals in the light of faith, (c) an opening of their shared life of faith to others by hospitality and encouragement in the Christian life, and (d) external critique and planning with respect to changing the social and environmental conditions that inhibit personal integrity and growth within the local community, the city, the nation, and the Church.

In each of these areas, the community will have to be present to itself: as fundamentally Christian in commitment and orientation; as counter-cultural in its advocacy of the Personal Form; as non-competitive in its encouraging, sustaining, and challenging; as corporately conscious of its most fundamental choices in faith and specific life options; as unified in its orientation to service, freedom, and the work of justice.

Such a communitarian life demands a commitment of

time, energy, and sacrifice. Its mutual support system cannot take place outside of a commonly recognized commitment of persons to each other in the name of their shared vision. A community of this kind must be (a) consciously choiceful, (b) explicitly committed to and willing to be called to the life of the Gospels, (c) open to change through the authentic living-out of its principles, and willing to be challenged to fuller Christian praxis, and (d) prepared to confront the patterns of the Commodity Form—injustice, manipulation, domination, dishonesty, escape—not only as they appear in the culture at large but also *as they surface within the group itself.*

In the process of sharing and deepening a living corporate faith, a Christian community will recognize that if it is not possible for a group of mutually committed men and women to struggle honestly with their own propensities to injustice, competition, and non-responsibility, they will hardly be justified in challenging those same patterns in the society at large which they criticize. They will realize that there is something fundamentally unjust in indicting other people or institutions for failing to do what they themselves refuse to undertake. This is the meaning of internal *and* external critique.

One's personal life, as well as the life of the community in which one lives, has social and political dimensions. That is true both in the sense that the communitarian life is in itself a stance and a witness against the Commodity Form, and in the sense that the same behaviors of domination and violence in international, national, and urban groups are potentially operative in a group of men and women who come together to foster and deepen their own Christian lives. If they are able to face and purify the patterns of injustice in their lives together, they will be able to bring greater compassion as well as insight to those patterns which are found at broader social and political levels.

MARRIAGE AND CELIBACY: COUNTER-CULTURAL LIFE CHOICES

Two dominant aspects of the gospel of commodity, as we have seen, are the erosion of permanent commitment and the thingification of human sexuality. While the media supposedly celebrate sexual liberation, sex in the media has no linkage with the full human person or human covenant. In this cultural ambience it becomes evident that the sexual life of Christians has considerable importance not only in their personal adherence to the Gospel of Jesus, but also in terms of witnessing to human personhood.

The only intimacy recognized in the Commodity Form is physical proximity. Knowledge of the other person as a person is painfully absent for many couples who enter marriage even though they may have considerable physical knowledge of each other. With the heightened hedonism of our culture, moreover, the pains of suffering and sacrifice are considered as impenetrable evils to be avoided at all cost. The continued intimacy of a shared life which is open to new life, however, is one which necessarily entails the suffering of growth and of daily dying to immediate gratification, to the satisfaction of one's clamoring ego, and to one's defenses against self-revelation. It is precisely in the fires of this struggle for love and commitment that marriages fall apart.

The high incidence of divorce cannot be separated from the dominant values of our society. The breakdown of familial covenant is part and parcel of the commodified universe, with its values of competition, hedonism, non-involvement, non-risk, loss of faith, and hopelessness. Many, even the most idealistic, enter the life choice of marriage with skepticism about their love, with paralyzing fears that it cannot last, and with lurking suspicions that they cannot give themselves unconditionally. And the very conditions and reservations they bring to the commitment actually determine the instability of it.

It is my belief that the institution of marriage (as well as the institutions which support its indissolubility against intense cultural propagandizing in the media) is one of the last bases for resistance to the Commodity Form. The family provides a primary sphere of human life where the deepest experiences of fidelity, of trust in other persons, of self-acceptance, of growth in intimacy, can occur and can offer data that belie the absolutes of capitalism. When families are broken apart, the incursion of the Commodity Form into the life of the child is even more far-reaching than otherwise. For a family-less child, the *only* data about life and love comes from media, social pressure, and cultural expectations. If covenantal marriage dissolves in this culture, the Personal Form may well disappear.

Part of the devaluation of the institution of marriage derives from the devaluation of human sexuality. The continually increasing incidence of pre-covenantal sexual intercourse among a majority of young people serves to separate the fullest expression of bodily intimacy from the interiority of total commitment and personal intimacy. Sexual intimacy receives both its intelligibility and its deepest eroticism from the intimacy of persons. Divorced from personal intimacy and the commitment upon which it is founded, sex itself becomes a social and personal lie. It is transformed into an object of immediate short-range gratification, in avoidance of the self-investment appropriate to a lifelong covenant and profound self-revelation. It is again quantity, often in different combinations and different packaging, which is substituted for the more fundamental longings of the human person.

In a culture which portrays life-commitment as impossible and undesirable, which inhibits the flowering of true intimacy, which deems a suffering love and sacrifice to be negative values, men and women who enter into a personal covenant by mature and free consent are taking a radical stance.

In an environment that intimidates persons who face risks made in freedom, that has reduced human affectivity to aggression, domination, and control, a life of marriage will be both terrifying and, at the same time, one of the most profound sources of liberation from the dialectic of domination and appropriation. It is a learning how to die, to accept one's finitude, to accept another person, to be stretched toward unconditional love, to truly share not only one's goods and gifts but one's poverty and life-grace.

In a society dedicated to "holding on to" everything, a life of marriage entered in the Personal Form is a schooling in how to give oneself away.

Sexuality and commitment as they are perceived through the Commodity Form provide the context wherein the issue of celibacy may be most fruitfully discussed. It is not surprising that in a culture which systematically attacks the covenant of marriage, the devaluation of other forms of chastity (I mean an integration of one's sexuality with one's whole personhood and life commitment) prevails. Chastity is impractical, out of date, undesirable.

The mutually sustaining forms of chastity in marriage and in the single life are yet to be fully investigated—especially the ways in which the struggles of celibate love are enhanced and nourished by the witness of faithful married love, and how the purifications and "dyings" of married love are complemented and sustained by men and women who live lives of celibate love. Both forms of chastity witness to the human condition and its full promise—one under the form of committed intimacy to another person and the risk of openness to new life, the other in a dimension of non-possessive loving and non-privatized care that is considered to be unacceptable foolishness in the canons of acculturated sexuality.

A celibate who lives a warm and affective life of intimacy which is not reducible to genitality, and a life of hope which is not reducible to the blood of offspring, says by this life-choice that human happiness, tenderness, compassion, and passion are made possible by our very humanness and a caring life of faith and hope. Such a life, of course, is more difficult in the doing than in the saying. It is true that there is great power in the witness of celibate love, in its implicit affirmation that one's personal choice has no intelligibility without eschatological faith and hope in Jesus Christ. In our culture especially, people have found it dumbfounding that someone might find human intimacy and compassion while foregoing physical fatherhood or motherhood and choosing to love without lover, spouse, or sexual gratification.

But it is also true that many celibates fail to give the ideal witness of the celibate life. The pains of relinquishment can be frequent and intense. The physical incompletions felt in intimacy without genital orientation or expression are filled with difficulties, purifications, and an aching vacuum close to the bottom of one's physical life. Care and carefulness are difficult to express in an integral way, and the sequential struggles found in a life of celibacy are as trying as the struggles in married love. There has been failure—not only in the high incidence of men and women who have rationalized their vowed public commitment in compromise and deceit, not only in those who have tried to change their commitment in openness and integrity, but also in the more culturally acceptable (and dangerous) forms of infidelity to celibate love. So often celibates have merely displaced their affective life rather than transforming it. Love and care are directed to things, possessions, games, professionalism, achievement, and the collection of trifles. A loss of tenderness and compassion, of affection and passion often seems to accompany the vowed celibate life. The concentration of all of one's moral sensitivity in moralistic sexual preoccupations may also be a by-product of a celibacy not grounded in love of Christ and of other human persons.

All of these risks and dangers, however, are worth taking, not only because of the intrinsic value that a life of celibate love can embody, but also and especially in the light of our culture's sexual gospel. Chastity, both in the marital and celibate forms, stands as a rare testimonial to human integrity, to the symbolic and actual importance of being embodied selves, to the preeminence of personhood and convenantal life. In the hedonistic culture, moreover, chastity is a most effective concrete critique of fulfillment through immediate gratification. It is a living refutation of the reduction of persons to either machines or animals, to progeny or to pleasure. The contradiction is well known. This is why sexual integrity is under such relentless attack in advanced Western societies, why it has to be explained away as deviance, repression, or frustration. It is a scandal to Madison Avenue, Hollywood, and the halls of academe and Rockdom. Yet it exists, and as a phenomenon within our culture, the life of married or celibate chastity can be a most subversive lived force today. It is truly counter-cultural.

The blind acceptance of the Commodity Form is especially evident in the realm of sexuality. Somehow we are led to believe that there is a sexual liberation going on—as if, mysteriously, human affectivity and sexuality were exempt from the hegemony of the thing. But if we look at sexuality and its mechanized commodification in our culture with any degree of honesty, we will see that this is not the case. The so-called sexual freedom is the affective erotic expression of the dominant economic and philosophical "reality" preached by our cultural gospel.

The wisdom of our capitalistic society in its marketing of sexuality and immediate gratification would have us believe that sexual integrity and commitment, chastity and marital fidelity, are something dreamed up by celibates in Rome hoping to impede our gratification and increase their control over us. The truth is, there is indeed a great deal of control over and manipulation of our sexuality, but it is not exercised by clerics. It is exercised by the market and the thing. There are societies and civilizations which never heard of the Roman Curia but which have insisted upon the importance of sexual integrity. But they have not been in the grips of a commodified universe and its overwhelming promotional power.

THE VOWED LIFE IN COMMUNITY: RESISTANCE TO INCULTURATION

In recent years most religious orders have been puzzled and frightened by the drop-off in the numbers of people applying for admittance. The only communities which seem to have grown are either those which have been heavily emphasizing traditional values, or those which, like Mother Teresa's Missionaries of Charity, have also made the investment of themselves in a life of unequivocal witness to the Gospel and service to the poor. In both of these cases there is an interesting phenomenon which is not too often looked at: each presents to a young person a *real alternative* to the gospel of the "world," a real possibility of living in a way not dictated by the lords of culture. In the case of sheer conservative emphases, the motivation could of course simply be the superficial distinctiveness of religious uniform, a rigorous rule, and formal singularity. It may also be a mere flight from the world and even from oneself. But it is quite clear that a way of life *different* from *passive acculturation* is sought. Most of the orders and congregations which have lost great numbers, or have even been disbanded, seem to have been the ones that have also foundered in finding their new identity in response to the call of the Church for renewal; in too many cases, change has been merely a move to further acculturation, secularism, and the adoption of cultural values.

I believe there are many alternatives to the superficial conservatism on one hand, and the panicky trendiness on the other. One powerful and often overlooked possibility is in the rediscovery of the religious life as a counter-cultural force. Men and women religious are called to be special Christian activists, who, by their subversive mode of life, invite other men and women to question the obsessions that dominate their social world and prevent them from being open to their own full potentiality as persons. "Religious" can live in the world, certainly, in continuity with the truly human, rooting themselves beneath and within various human projects—economic, educative, social, political, and ecclesiastical—with the aim of liberating themselves and others for mobilization into deeper Christian life. Nonetheless, by the quality and intensity of their prayer and shared communal lives, they will witness to the fact that the human condition is not reducible to social and political projects. Their lives will clearly point to values that transcend the limits of nation, race, class, or ideology, and that sustain their commitment to each human effort they undertake. A covenant with and in Christ remains central to their vows, but the very *evangelical* nature of their commitments leads them to be culturally radical.

In their openness to one another, in their fidelity to the Word of God, in their renunciation of dominating power—even though isolation might be less demanding, infidelity less precarious, and power more immediately satisfying—religious have the opportunity to bear unambiguous witness to *faith,* founded in the God who invites. They choose *obedience* to God's calling forth of their personhood, expressing it in fidelity to their Christian tradition, to their life promise, and to their common struggles.

In their relinquishment of private property and its accumulation, in their rejection of self-aggrandizement and all forms of psychological or economic possessiveness—even though extensive property is the aspiration of our culture, and aggrandizement the promise of material fulfillment—religious have the opportunity to witness unambiguously to *hope,* grounded in the God who shares. They choose to be *poor* by letting go of final reliance upon possessions and by a trusting abandonment to the Lord.

In the risky gift of their lives and the vulnerability of their self-divestment in compassion—even though self-withholding seems the guarantee of security, and dispassionate coolness the model of cultural isolation—religious have the opportunity to bear unambiguous witness to *love* grounded in the God who gives. They choose to be single-mindedly *chaste* in the passionate gift of their whole selves without reservation.

We can see, then, how the traditional vows of poverty, chastity, and obedience are not only expressions of a life of faith, hope, and love, not only fundamental commitments to human freedom, but also relentlessly counter-cultural stances in the three crucial areas of human action. It will be well to elaborate on this.

In the area of property, capitalist culture offers human fulfillment under the guise of infinite accumulation, appropriation, and competitive self-enhancement. The vow of poverty is a stance taken in freedom not against property *per se,* but against security and fulfillment in property. It is not a negation of things, it is an affirmation of their proper ordering in human relations: persons always before property. Men and women cannot be fulfilled, saved, or made happy by the production or accumulation of commodities. They are fulfilled only when they relinquish their idols, only when they see things as *expressions,* and servants of personhood. The vow of poverty emphasizes detachment, simplicity, sharing, and a celebration of the goods of the earth. In each emphasis, the vow then embodies a value-stand against cultural dogma. At the same time, it is also a solid foundation for social activism, rooted in the conviction that the human person is primary in ethical, political, and economic life; thence follow the moral imperatives of equity, the fair distribution of wealth, the obligation to help the poor and dispossessed, and the desirability of communitarianism. The vow of poverty is the theoretical and practical controlling limit on our relation to property and things. Religious life demands it as a bulwark of its fidelity and promise. But our culture needs it even more desperately.

The second major area of human interaction is in the

issue of power. We have seen how this issue is resolved by the cultural gospel, with its emphasis upon *laissez faire* marketing and morality, upon isolation and individualism, upon domination, control, and competition. The vow of obedience professes that isolation and egocentrism, as well as the violence that arises from them, will not rule one's life or one's community. It is a purification of the ego's demands for self-sufficiency. Obedience is a commitment to resolve human struggles not through domination, but through openness to the other and a yielding of one's "non-negotiable demands." Obedience is the willingness to be named, to be called, and to be held responsible as an interdependent social being.

The final crucial area of the counter-cultural stance of the religious vows is human affectivity. Not only is this area repressed in the Commodity Form; it is also displaced, by the reduction of human sexuality to mechanics and disspirited coupling. Musculature displaces passion. Love is a production, a making, a making it. It is a performance and a drive to legitimation. Commitment is evaded, as we have seen, and the purifications of our desires and affections never take place. Rather, they are channeled into the seductions of escape, violence, and manipulation. The vow of chastity, on the other hand, professes human interiority and the trans-cultural, trans-temporal sacredness of the human body. Letting go of the immortality of blood, it affirms the eternality of Love. It is an exercise of free disengagement from cultural imperatives; it is a declaration of independence from the devaluation not only of sexuality, but of personhood itself.

In each of these basic areas—power, property, and affectivity—the person who lives the vowed life finds himself or herself in radical opposition to the values of the culture. In each area, moreover, we have a social and political programmatic, an alternative model of human interaction and growth, a foundational model for entering and changing the cultural ambient. Sharing. The primacy of persons over property. Responsibility in a mutually accepted interdependence. Human loving. The elevation of sexuality to a human act.

So many men and women who live the traditional religious life of the vows do not make such connections. Traditionalist groups fail to draw any relationship between the life they profess to live and its socio-political impact. They often present themselves as political quietists with personal and corporate financial security.

More reformed groups have succeeded only in passing themselves off as accomplished "men and women of the world." What special gift do they have to offer? They are not perceived as a challenge to or hope for the desperation of our society. And often, uninformed by prayer, asceticism, or passionate spirit, they perceive themselves as secularists with little to live or say. In both cases, the powerful content of the three vows is neither perceived nor practiced.

In this instance, religious men and women fail to touch the energetic sources of their vocation. And it is precisely this misconnection which underlies the ineffectual changes that have been attempted. Only when we see ourselves as social and cultural beings who have chosen a gospel other than the one offered by culture itself can we discover our full vigorous potentialities and make the changes that are incumbent upon us. Only then can we see the necessity for a life of integrity in our sexual lives, a life of authentic sharing, simplicity, and detachment in our use of things, and a life of true responsibility and commitment in obedience.

We are witnessing, perhaps now more than ever, an

increasing demand for a more explicit presence of Christian communities and their living of the life of the Gospels and evangelical counsels. The need is even more pressing when situated in a civilization that grows continuously more materialistic, individualistic, and consumption-oriented, more technologically trapped, more mechanistic in its affectivity and more fragmented in its long-range life commitments.

If my reading of our culture is correct, the last thing desirable for religious people is an easy identification with such a culture. The last thing needed is another milieu-culture Christian or milieu-culture community. Christianity indeed must be lived in space and time within cultures—but always beyond the culture, transcending it and transforming it, and if necessary working against its values as a counter-cultural force. The life of the traditional vows is an attempt at an admittedly limited "unambiguous statement" about fulfillment of persons in non-appropriation, in a love which is not reducible to genitality or mechanistic sexuality, and in a committed life of mutually shared risk and openness to the other.

We presently experience a growing awareness, on the part of many young persons, of the desirability of and necessity for a shared community of prayer, vision, support, and resistance to the idols of capitalism. Many young people are recognizing that their faith, hope, and love have to be made explicit and embodied in community consciousness and action. Yet these people find little of the direction and leadership they seek. They look for the encouragement of lived witness and invitation, but the lived witness is too often ambivalent, too often like the culture itself; and the invitations are too often hidden, too often timid.

At the same time, a considerable number of men and

women who have embraced the life of traditional vows and community are experiencing a call to a personal and communal rebirth as Christians. They desire to have their faith and vows more radicalized and centrally focused upon the Gospels and the person of Christ. They experience this call not so much as a judgment upon the past as a judgment upon their own future.

Moreover, there is a growing need for mediation in the Church and in society, due to increasing polarization, incapacity for tolerance, and the instability of men and women in their life promises. It has to be questioned whether the present structures of the parish and religious houses are truly capable of meeting these polarizations and challenges. Perhaps a more intense communal life of prayer, celebration, and service is the most appropriate response. But there is little leadership available and few viable models of community life are offered. In response to such a situation, it would be well to consider whether traditional communities could see their mission as providing models for corporate living and sharing which are less culturally ambiguous and more open to the larger church around them.

Many communities of religious in their training live in large buildings (even though they might be divided into smaller subgroups) that tend to separate their members from other people, because of environmental necessity or for the sake of efficiency or academic efficacy. Many undesirable possibilities emerge: isolated personal lives, irresponsible and dishonest attitudes toward poverty, anonymous security and abundance, unresponsiveness to communal needs or excessive waste, and assumption of leisure-class values and aspirations, with ignorance of critical social issues and decisions (racial prejudice, abortion, militarism, media exploitation, penal reform, urban decay). These are often the by-products of isolation, suffocating comfort, and false security.

After the completion of religious formation a person often tends to find self-definition in terms of an institution, a school, or a professional task. Sharing frequently takes place on this level alone—students, classes, projects. Sharing of faith, doubts, communal strategy, decision-making, mutual encouragement, and correction become privatized and increasingly infrequent. What is neglected, because it is taken for granted and rarely made explicit, is the fact that faith and the life of vows rooted in Christ are the only sustaining bases of corporate identity and personal meaning.

Moreover, the institutional frames themselves tend to separate religious men and women from other people. A religious faculty as a community of service and faith rarely shares its life with the lay faculty even to the simple extent of sharing meals with them, Eucharistic or other. Rarely are outsiders regularly invited to pray with the religious community. The houses take on the appearance of closed fortresses; at least that is the way they are frequently—albeit sometimes unjustly—perceived. Community life can become so closed as never to have a basis for sharing lived faith with fellow professionals, students, friends, or even members within the community. What is shared is knowledge, professional competence, even ministerial powers—but rarely the intimacy of a life lived in faith and hope.

In some unfortunate moves toward smaller communities, none of the difficulties above are really transcended; rather they are transposed merely into another smaller, more private, more secularized, more comfortable environment. What we lack in these cases—as in our dying large communities—is a model of communal life that emerges from a cultural and social understanding of the meaning of the vows in a lived atheistic culture. What we lack is a vision of community life which is apostolic in the very offering to society of an alternative way of living and being together. What we lack is an insight into the dialectical relationship between faith and society.

Religious communities, in their effort to renew themselves, miss the power of their own traditions and the vows when they search for ways to make life more amenable and luxurious, or more isolated and rigidly formal, or more cozy and undemanding. An understanding of how the Commodity Form has insinuated itself into both the conservative and the modern models of community might serve to unleash the full potential of communities of men and women who openly testify to a personal and corporate living out of the Gospel of Jesus Christ. Too often religious life has been and remains a testimonial to affluence, financial survival, isolation, and individualism—the hallmarks of the Commodity Form way of life. It need not be that way. But it will be otherwise only if we so choose—newly conscious of the cultural and social context of lived faith.

THE COMMODITY FORM	THE PERSONAL FORM
Value Grounded in Thinghood	*Value Grounded in Personhood*
Marketability of the person	Intrinsic value of persons
Production: worth as what you do	Worth as who you are
Consumption	Self-Gift
Thing-Knowledge	*Personal Knowledge*
Observation and description	Faith: self-consciousness and interiority
Measurement and control	Understanding and trust
Quality as quantity	Human quality as non-measurable
Emphasis on derived knowledge	Immediate experience
How questions	Why-questions
Thing-Willing	*Personal-Willing*
Determinism	Limited freedom
Escape	Self-investment
Non-commitment	Covenant
Thing-Behavior	*Person-Behavior*
Violence:	Peace:
Domination	Acceptance of weakness
Manipulation	Respect of freedom
Retaliation	Forgiveness
Punishment	Healing
Defense	Defenselessness
Devaluation of Life	Exaltation of least person
Demand	Invitation
Competition	Sharing
Retention	Giving

THE COMMODITY FORM	THE PERSONAL FORM
Thing-Like Affectivity	*Personal Affectity*
Sexuality as mechanics	Sexuality as sign of person
Body as machine	Body as temple— sacral presence
Fear/threat	Fear not
Non-commitment	Covenant—committed devotedness
Retention of self	Self-donation
Technique	Telos
Externality	Interiority
Replaceability	Uniqueness
Coolness	Tenderness
Hardness	Compassion
Accumulation	Detachment
Invulnerability	Vulnerability
Exchange	Prodigal love
Hedonism: immediate self-gratification	Generosity: suffering love
Thing-Reality	*Person-Reality*
Having	Being
What is	What we can be
Human skepticism	Faith and fidelity
Human paralysis and doubt	Hope and trust
Individual isolation	Love
Unfreedom as final condition	Freedom as final condition
Death	Life

Celibacy and Community

Jerome Murphy-O'Connor, O.P.

Although a definite improvement on previous authoritative statements, what Vatican II has to say about religious celibacy is still far from satisfying, because it concentrates exclusively on what celibacy means for the individual religious. In *Perfectae caritatis,* no. 12, there is only a passing reference to community: "Above all, everyone should remember—superiors especially—that chastity has stronger safeguards in a community where true fraternal love reigns among its members." This statement carries the clear implication that community has no intrinsic relationship to celibacy; common-life is no more than a convenient way for an individual to live out his commitment. I don't believe that the Council intended this implication, and so the ambiguity of the statement demands an explanation. I suggest that the ambiguity was motivated by a desire not to draw too clear a distinction between the celibacy of the religious and that of the secular priest. A reading of the Council documents manifests that there is no substantial difference between what is said of priestly celibacy (*Optatam totius,* no. 10; *Presbyterorum ordinis,* no. 16) and of religious celibacy (*Perfectae caritatis,* no. 12), so that commentators feel free to use the data contained in all three texts in order to create a uniform synthesis. In this one can detect the intention not to play into the hands of those who opposed priestly celibacy. To stress the intrinsic relation between celibacy and community, it was thought, would have been to weaken the position of those who wanted to maintain priestly celibacy, a position already gravely compromised by the admission that there was no intrinsic relationship between priesthood and celibacy. Paradoxically, the reverse is in fact true, and one of the strongest arguments for priestly celibacy emerges from an analysis of his place in the parish community. It is not my intention to develop this point here, but what can be said can be inferred rather easily from what will be said regarding religious celibacy and community.

THE NEW TESTAMENT

The classical New Testament passage cited as the basis for the vocation to celibacy is Matthew 19:12:

> There are eunuchs who have been so from birth, and there are eunuchs who have been made eunuchs by men, and there are eunuchs who have made themselves eunuchs for the sake of the Kingdom of heaven. He who is able to receive this, let him receive it.

There is an allusion to this text at the very beginning of *Perfectae caritatis,* no. 12. Fortunately the reference is very discreet, because this passage has nothing to do with celibacy in the sense of the decree. This statement, attributed to Jesus by Matthew alone, is in response to the disciples'

objection (19:10) occasioned by Jesus' ruling that marriage after divorce is adultery (19:9 equals Mark 10:11–
12). It must, therefore, be understood in the perspective
of the preceding discussion regarding marriage and divorce, and this permits only one interpretation. The text
concerns the fidelity that is demanded of the abandoned
partner in a marriage that has broken up. Marriage is the
total gift of self to another. The commitment is mutual,
but the radicalism of Christian love means that if one partner defaults the other is not freed. The totality of self-giving means the acceptance of the possibility of throwing
away one's life for the other. This is accepted as entirely
natural as long as the two partners are faithful to each other, and history contains many examples of husbands and
wives who have willingly sacrificed themselves for each
other. Christian love is much more exigent, and does not
accept the faithlessness of one as sufficient justification for
the other to break the original commitment. It must continue faithful, even when there is no human possibility of
response. This is the living death of the eunuch which the
abandoned partner must accept "for the sake of the Kingdom." In other words, by accepting enforced celibacy as
the permanent possibility of return and forgiveness for the
sinner, the abandoned partner witnesses to the altruistic
character of Christian love, and manifests that he is truly a
follower of Christ who "died for us when we were yet sin-
ners." "Why, one will hardly die for a just man, though
perhaps for a good man one will dare even to die. But
God shows his love for us in that while we were yet sin-
ners Christ died for us" (Rom 5:6–8). Thus, although
Matthew 19:12 is not concerned with freely-chosen celibacy, it says much about the radical character of genuinely
Christian commitment in love.

It is in such radicalism that the New Testament roots of chosen celibacy are to be discerned. Nothing more concrete or more specific is to be found in the New Testament, but I think we can gain a valuable insight if we compare two texts which are not normally looked at together. Both appear in the Gospel of Matthew:

He who loves his father or mother more than me is not worthy of me; and he who loves son or daughter more than me is not worthy of me (*10:37; cf. 19:29*).

And stretching out his hand toward his disciples, he said: "Here are my mother and my brothers. For whoever does the will of my Father in heaven is my brother, and sister, and mother" (*12:49–50*).

The first text appears in another form in Luke 14:26: "If anyone comes to me and does not hate his own father and mother and *wife* and children and brothers and sisters, yes, and even his own life, he cannot be my disciple." In biblical usage the "hate" of Luke is equivalent in meaning to the "love more" of Matthew. No mention is made of "wife" in Matthew, and this accords with the above interpretation of the eunuch-saying. The fundamental message is identical in both, and is parallel to what Jesus said to the rich young man. If affective ties interfere with commitment to Christ they must be abandoned. Were it not for the second text one might be tempted to infer from this that commitment to Christ could mean a life without affective bonds. Jesus, however, also makes it clear that commitment to him is the discovery of affective ties that did not hitherto exist. In the act of faith the believer becomes part of a community of love.

WHY CHOSEN CELIBACY?

Every Christian, however, is called to this renunciation and to this community. Yet not every Christian is called to voluntary celibacy. Why, then, are some so called? The only answer has to be inferred from the two texts juxtaposed above. The relationship of love that may have to be renounced is *different* from the relationship of love into which we enter with Christ, and the proclamation of the Gospel demands that this difference be brought to the attention of the world. What precisely this difference is cannot be adequately specified in cold analytic categories, but this is irrelevant because the Christian is not asked to explain this new possibility of loving but to live it.

To love without adequate motivation, to love without hope of return, seems impossible to most men. They would like to believe because it would give immeasurably greater depth and richness to human life, but it appears as pure idealism, beautiful but completely impractical. They may be briefly inspired by an eloquent presentation of this ideal, but the only presentation that will really touch their hearts is the existential affirmation of this love in a consistent life-style.

By their baptism all Christians are called to give to the world this lived demonstration of the "newness" of the love manifested by Christ. It is supposed to be their distinctive characteristic, both individually and collectively.

> A new commandment I give to you, that you love one another; even as I have loved you, that you also love one another. By this all men will know that you are my disciples, if you have love for one another (*Jn 13:34–35*).

What is new here is not simply the primacy given to the precept of charity, but the standard that is indicated. It must be a love as generous and as universal as the sacrificial love of Christ. The impact of such love has been well underlined by Tertullian's ironic remark: "It is especially this exercise of charity that has given us a bad character in the eyes of many. See, they say, how they love one another! Because they [i.e. the pagans] hate one another. See, they say, how they are ready to die for each other! Because they [i.e. the pagans] are ready rather to kill each other" (*Apolog.*, 19:7). And Minutius Felix commented: "They love each other even before they come to know each other" (*Octavius*, 9:2). Could a Christian apologist today, without ridicule, put the same observation in the mouth of an adversary?

Absolutely speaking, celibacy is not necessary to the existential demonstration of the "newness" of Christian love. Married love is intended to extend to all others in the Christian community with the same intensity as is shown to members of the family. Theoretically, it is fully capable of having the same impact as celibate love. The operative word here is "theoretically," because in the practical order the situation is very different, and it is on this level that witness is effective. Celibate love has a greater witness value than married love, because it is less ambiguous. Marriage is a natural institution, and love of great intensity and dedication can and does exist in marriages that make no claim to be Christian. The witness value of Christian married love, therefore, is diminished by the difficulty of distinguishing the natural from the genuinely Christian. In other words, it is too easy to explain away. The outsider is not immediately impressed or disturbed by the presence of something "new." In certain cases the superhuman dimension of Christian married love may be inescapable, for example, in the fidelity and devotion shown to a partner who is a permanent invalid, but this is irrelevant in the perspective of a theology of witness which must of necessity concern itself with the ordinary case and with normal situations. This is not intended as a disparagement of married love. It is in no way inferior to celibate love. Christian marriage is rooted in the same faith and hope that inspires religious life. However, from the point of view of witness we have to place ourselves in the position of the outsider. Motives do not impinge on his perception unless a life-style translates them into the domain of sensible reality. Married love does this less effectively than celibate love simply because it permits more alternative explanations. The presence of a partner obscures the commitment to the ideal, because the outsider can find familiar explanations to account for such love, sex, companionship, support, etc.

The parish and the diocese are intended to be true communities, but each is made up of family units which in themselves are communities. The married Christian, therefore, of necessity belongs to *two* communities, the family and the local church. In practice the edges of the distinction between the two are inevitably blurred, and no one can tell whether he is sustained by the natural love of the family or the "new" love of the Christian community. In times of crisis the married Christian can move both consciously and unconsciously from one community to the other. When the Church fails him he can turn to the family, and when the family fails him he can turn to the Church. It is this fluidity that detracts from the witness value of married love, no matter how profoundly Christian it may be.

The celibate, on the other hand, belongs to only one community. In opposition to the parish, this microcosm of the Church is not made up of smaller communities, but of individuals. In this sense it is an ultimate community like the family, but it is not bound by any ties of blood. Since all the members are sexually normal adults of the same sex, the mere fact of its existence forces the mind of the outsider to seek the motivation for its existence. None of his normal standards of judgment apply. He cannot fit the religious community into any of his habitual categories. It is precisely because of its ability to produce this effect that the witness value of celibate love is superior to that of married love, because the essence of witness is to force outsiders off balance in such a way that they are obliged to ask the crucial question, "What makes them different?" This is confirmed by the simple fact of experience that outsiders show much more curiosity about religious communities than about Christian marriages. I would even go so far as to say that the witness value of married love depends on the witness given by celibate love, in the sense that it is only when the outsider has been alerted by a celibate community to the "newness" of Christian love that he can discern the much more subtle signs of this love in a Christian marriage.

CELIBACY AND COMMUNITY

Despite what has been said above it does not follow that every religious community gives greater witness than every Christian marriage. Some families are a much more effective proclamation of the Gospel than many religious communities. The point that I have been making is that in itself celibate love has a greater witness potential than married love. Hence, it has a necessary function in the Christian community. Whether this potential is always effectively realized is a separate question to which we must now turn.

It is often said that in virtue of the vow of celibacy the religious is freed to love, and this theme is taken up by the Council documents when they speak of celibacy. With regard to religious the formulation is a little discreet, because it says only that celibacy is "a most suitable way for religious to spend themselves readily in God's service and in works of the apostolate" (*Perfectae caritatis,* no. 12). This could mean a number of things, but the mind of the Council is clearly indicated in the passage concerning priestly celibacy: "They more freely devote themselves in him and through him to the service of God and men" (*Presbyterorum ordinis,* no. 16). Such an understanding of celibacy not only ignores the realities of life, but is in conflict with the common-sense attitude of the traditional teaching on the hierarchy of charity. In maintaining that the primary obligation of charity concerns those who are closest to us St. Thomas quotes both Paul and Augustine (II-II, q. 26). According to the former, "If anyone does not provide for his relatives, and especially for his own family, he has denied the faith and is worse than an unbeliever" (1 Tim 5:8). This idea is generalized by Augustine, "Since it is impossible to be useful to all, you should give preference to those who are closest to you by reason of circumstances of time or place or for any other reason" (*Doct. Christ.,* I, 28). The religious is no freer than a married person. If a husband or wife is limited by the concern he or she is obliged to manifest for his or her family, the religious is limited in precisely the same way by concern for the community. It is an unfortunate paradox, but the idea that celibacy frees for universal love is one of the major reasons why religious communities have failed to fulfill their witness potential, because inevitably this gives rise to the view that the community is merely a base *from which* the real work is done. The result is that religious communities become loveless deserts. Not only does this make celibacy virtually impossible because men cannot live without love, but it means that the outsider who is shocked into asking "What makes them different?" finds nothing but a verbal answer to his question. The real answer, the existential answer, is lacking. Not unnaturally, then, celibate life is judged to be meaningless. If religious life produces shock as an immediate reaction, it must also appeal when it is looked into more deeply, and it does this only when the quality of life in a celibate community speaks to the buried desire of all men for totality and completeness.

Celibacy is but another facet of the reciprocity that we have seen to be characteristic of the vow of poverty. In poverty we give all to the community and receive all on the level of the means of material subsistence. Similarly in celibacy we give all to the community and receive all on the level of affective life. Just as the community meets our material needs, so it must also meet our affective needs. Just as the religious is productive in material terms, so he must also be productive in affective terms. These two areas cover the fundamental needs of humanity. Without bread and love man cannot live. Consequently there is a very profound reason why poverty and celibacy were chosen as the structural elements of religious life. They manifest, in the two domains with which all men must be concerned, the shared being-in-Christ which is the essence of Christian life. The fraternal charity that should animate common-life is not simply a safeguard for celibacy, it is an integral part of the witness that is given by celibacy.

COMMUNITY LIFE

We have seen that the *raison d'être* of celibacy is on the level of witness. It is also a sacrifice "for the sake of the Kingdom," in the sense that the Kingdom of God may be manifested as unambiguously as possible as a community in which men are loved not for what they are but for what they can become.

The real danger for celibates is not the build-up of a sexual tension that cannot be controlled, but the suppression or deflection of the affective powers. They are stifled if the celibate avoids the stress and tensions of deep interpersonal relations. In any religious community, no matter how committed and how sincere the members, there will be such tensions, because it is a formation-community in which perfection is only the goal striven for, not a condition of membership. We strive to be all "spirit" but, as Paul was well aware, the "flesh" is still active. Even in a community where all are sincerely striving to let the Spirit dominate, emotional tensions will accumulate to the point where a flash of passion is the inevitable result. Since a religious community is supposed to be a community of peace, the recurrence of such explosions worries many. Sometimes a guilt complex develops, and an attempt is made to eradicate the root of such tensions by withdrawal to a more superficial level of involvement in the community. The unfortunate result is that the personality becomes sterile, because its life is nothing more than a protective system of evasion and compromise. If this happens all the witness value of that life vanishes. It is not necessary that it should happen. It should be recognized that emotional tensions are a concomitant of human living, and that a good row between relatively mature individuals is a very healthy thing. It might help to recall that both Jesus in the episode of the money-changers in the temple, and Paul in the Corinthian letters, discharged their inner tensions in passionate outbursts of extreme violence. In a formation-community an explosion of passion is an essential ingredient in conversion. Not only does it lead to deeper self-knowledge, but in the aftermath one sees new opportunities for love. Both Jesus and Paul compare Christians to "children," and a small child is the only human being who reacts with instinctive honesty in interpersonal relations. What is praised in the child is this simplicity, not the lack of control that often accompanies it. Maturity is the acquisition of the necessary controls but care must be taken—and this is especially true of the celibate—that honesty remain intact. By any standards sincerity and honesty, both of which imply courage, are essential ingredients in a life capable of commanding respect and admiration.

The alternative to the suppression of affective powers is to permit them to be deflected, either to "things" or to persons outside the community. The celibate's life can all too easily become centered on substitutes such as art, research, administration, or a project. If one is successful the resulting acclaim can meet the need for affective love. Should this happen the reciprocity that is integral to the witness of celibacy is destroyed, because the member no longer lives *from* the affective life of the community. There is no lasting satisfaction in this way, and failure often reveals a trading mentality. Having, he thinks, given himself entirely to God, the religious feels that he is owed certain satisfactions. When these are not forthcoming, because the whole idea is false, bitterness and cynicism are the result. This phenomenon is frequent when community is conceived simply as a base, and celibacy is thought of in terms of service. Celibacy is certainly for service, not the service of *doing,* but the service of *loving.* Actions, of course, are involved, but the error lies in considering them as primary. The intensity of love with which they are infused is the only thing that really matters.

The witness value of celibacy is much less seriously weakened if the affective powers are focused on persons outside the community, because celibate love is obviously meant to overflow the rather narrow limits of a community. A danger for the witness value of celibacy arises only if and when the affective *center* of the religious' life is displaced outside the community, because at that point he ceases to live from the community affectively, and the tangible evidence of the reciprocity of Christian being is destroyed. A second danger then becomes imminent. Psychic energy is limited, and it is naturally channeled in a give-and-take relationship. If the affection needed to live humanly comes from outside the community, it is inevitable that the affective powers of the religious will also be channeled in that direction, thus leaving the rest of the community less to live on. Psychic capital cannot be measured as accurately as money, but the analogy is not too remote. Unless all the members of the community produce to the limits of their affective capacity, the quality of the community's life—which is its *raison d'être*—will diminish.

The most subtle way in which this can happen is the religious' involvement with the various generations of his own family. In itself such involvement is a good thing, because without such contacts the best of communities become claustrophobic, and it is a human need to be able to stand back at moments and look at community with the perspective given by distance and a point of comparison. The difficulties of family life are such as to provide a most effective deterrent to the idea that religious are the only

group to have troubles and tensions. Moreover, an awareness of the roles being worked out in a family can permit a
religious to detect infantile attitudes in what is supposed
to be a community of mature adults. However, these (and
many other) positive advantages, when reinforced by the
claim of blood, can bring a religious to the point where he
(or she) knows his nieces and nephews better than the
youngest members of his community. At this point it is
clear that more of himself (time, thought, energy) is being
given to those outside than to those inside the community.

From a theological point of view the problem of
friendship with a member of the opposite sex is identical
with the problem of overinvolvement with one's own family. It is governed by the same principle, and it carries the
same built-in danger. Unfortunately, however, the danger
implicit in this type of relationship is most often exagger-
ated to the point that such friendship is considered incompatible with celibacy. Such a reaction is one-sided, because
this relationship has as many positive aspects as involvement with one's own family. Real maturity (which is indis-
pensable to witness) demands that an individual be able to
relate to both sexes. This ability cannot be acquired in a
vacuum. It is also a fact of experience that individuals
learn infinitely more about themselves through friendship
with a member of the opposite sex than through contacts
with their own sex. The former carries with it an intensity
lacking in the latter because of the natural complementarity of the two sexes, and unless confronted with this intensity an individual can remain completely unaware of the
strengths and weaknesses of his own character. In far too
many communities the view prevails that celibacy is a pre-
cious jewel that has to be "protected" from tarnishment,
and as a result contact with the opposite sex is reduced to
the minimum. This is particularly true of female commu-

nities. This view involves two completely erroneous assumptions, namely, that women are somehow weaker than men, and that witness is given simply by the fact of having taken a vow of celibacy. This latter assumption is but a facet of the effort, which I have already criticized, to shift the burden of witness from the personal to the institutional. Anyone who still accepts the former assumption would do well to read D. S. Bailey's *The Man–Woman Relation in Christian Thought* (London, 1959) in order to fully appreciate the absurdity of the only reasons theologians could find to support the hypothesis that women are inferior to men. Such "protectionism" is a much greater impediment to the witness value of a celibate community than any excess in an individual relationship, because it keeps the members in a state of immaturity which diminishes the quality of their lives. Scandal will also be invoked as an argument against any friendship between religious of different sexes. Given the contemporary situation it is undeniable that there will be "talk," but this does not mean that true scandal is given. The laity are so badly informed regarding the true nature of celibacy that such scandal can only be classed as "pharisaical." And traditionally the danger of pharisaic scandal is no impediment to a course of action. It is also a fact of experience that such "talk" disappears when such friendships are accompanied, not by a leap over the wall, but by a marked improvement in the quality of community life. Once such a climate has been established individual excesses are understood to be nothing more than an error of judgment on the part of an immature individual. It must also be recognized that the hypercritical attitude of some so-called Christians forces such friendships into channels that they would not normally take in an atmosphere permeated by genuinely Christian trust and understanding.

To sum up: Celibacy is not freedom from responsibilities. It is just as much a commitment to responsibility in community as is marriage. The communities, of course, are different, but that is the whole point. The *raison d'être* of the celibate community is that its reciprocal love should be so manifest as to inspire a similar self-sacrificing love in the family (where, for example, the natural bond is often sundered by the generation gap) and in the wider community made up of family units. The necessity for celibacy is the practical one of contemporary need. People want to be *shown,* not told, that a love unshadowed by any possibility of selfishness does result in a more human person. They need the demonstration that a community of love is possible among those who are bound by no ties of blood. In choosing celibacy the religious assumes the responsibility of answering one of the most fundamental questions of contemporary man.

Will the New Church Need Celibates?

DAVID M. KNIGHT

ONE OF MY FAVORITE cousins is a no-nonsense Catholic. When the new assistant in his parish urged the congregation one Sunday morning to exchange the peace of Christ with one another, his wife turned to him with knowledge in her eye and said, "Do you want me to give you the kiss of peace?" His answer expressed the sentiments of the congregation more truthfully, I would guess, than any other formula of the Mass: "You do and I'll kick you right out in the aisle!"

Catholics just aren't used to the idea that they go to Mass to be with anybody. They go to fulfill their duty toward God, to receive Communion if they are fervent, and to hear something helpful in the sermon if they are lucky. But the idea of the Mass as a gathering of people who have something to share with one another is new to them; at the Mass each gets his share of grace directly from God, or at best through the priest, and everyone goes home as unrelated to his fellow Christians as he was when he came.

What this amounts to saying is that what we call the "local Christian community" is very seldom a community and even more seldom a community based on Christianity. Where "community" exists in the normal parish it is formed through Bingo and bazaars, and its focus is more likely to be the Catholic school than God or the Gospel of Jesus Christ. It is not in church or in what the Scriptures call their weekly "assembly" that Catholics get to know each other or experience a common bond; it is in working together on some project to finance a para-evangelical activity of the parish: a new building, a picnic for the altar boys, new uniforms for the grade school team. When you find a Catholic who feels he "belongs" in his local parish community, you can pretty safely guess he has a knack for raising money or helping others to raise it. In what we call the "local church," community is built around practical needs, not around a common experience of the transforming grace of Jesus Christ.

If we ask where celibates fit into this picture, the answer most Catholics give would point to the practical economy of having unfamilied priests and sisters to take on the work of the parish. Everyone wants sisters—to run the Catholic school. That these sisters are unmarried is a financial asset, but of no particular religious significance except to demonstrate what lengths of sacrifice some people will accept in order to do the work of the Kingdom of God. And parents are grateful, because the Kingdom of God in this instance provides them with a relatively low-cost alternative to the public school system with its disciplinary problems and its—let us be honest—indiscriminate racial integration.

If this is what celibacy means—and too often the celibates themselves can give no deeper explanation—then celibacy's contribution to the local Christian community is just to give accent to the functional, this-worldly, service-oriented, practical image of the Catholic Church. Celibates boost everyone's morale, because to them the schools and the hospitals and all the other services provided by the Catholic Church in this world, and for the good life in this world, are worth the sacrifice of even such a personal value as marriage. It's comforting to know that the "best," most self-sacrificing representatives of Gospel-response agree that the institutions and the establishment are what Christianity is all about. (And it is correspondingly upsetting when these same representative Christians hit the picket line, calling the status quo into question. In this case the witness is still the same: Christianity at the service of a more human life in this world, but the witnesses are on the side of the opposition party.)

What we have to ask here is whether the whole message of celibacy is being missed—by celibates and non-celibates alike. And to ask this we must ask very soberly whether, in the average parish church, the message of Christianity itself is still unheard.

The whole message of celibacy (according to Karl Rahner, S.J. in "The Theology of Renunciation," *Theological Investigations III,* p. 47) is that the focus of man's fulfillment is now outside the world. Man's good, his only true good, his completely satisfying good, does not come from within this intramundane sphere, but from outside of creation. This is not to say that man is waiting for "pie in the sky when you die." A spirituality that is eschatological in this sense would give no importance to this world or to man's time in it, but would place all of life's true value chronologically after death. But Christianity is eschatological in the sense that the eschaton, the final state of things, is already a present reality: through baptism man dies and rises again right now, in this life, and possesses eternal life as a member of the living Christ. Through grace man shares right now in the life of God, and three

Persons abide in him. Thus man's fulfillment is here, but it is not from here. His real good is in the world (in his own heart), but it is from beyond this world, and nothing that is from this world can give it or take it away.

How celibacy proclaims this message we will develop later. At present we point out that this is also the core of the Gospel proclamation: that Jesus Christ is risen and real, and as present and available in his own person to his followers today as he was during his life upon earth. The first Christian assemblies were a celebration of the presence of Christ. They were "Eucharist," thanksgiving for the presence of the Lord—the redemptive, saving, triumphant presence of the Christ who was immolated and who rose victorious over sin and death to unite all men in himself in the new life he came to pour out in abundance upon the earth. When the early Christians gathered together secretly in houses before the first light of dawn, to read the Scriptures, praise God with one another, and pray for the needs of the brotherhood throughout the world, the focal point of their gathering was the eucharistic Christ. The real presence of the Lord gave to the word of Christ that was read and to the body of Christ that was assembled an authentic stamp of present identification with Jesus of Nazareth. Jesus the Lord was risen; Jesus was present among them in his own real body. Therefore the word that was read and the body that was assembled were still the expression of the living Lord, the unique and personal Jesus, Son of God.

The first Christians literally gathered together out of darkness to celebrate the light of Christ still burning among them. In the darkness of night, and out of the surrounding darkness of paganism, they came together to gather around the light of his word, and to share the light reflected in their hearts. And where they gathered together, Jesus the light of the world became present also, in the transformation of the bread and wine, to leave no doubt where the light of the word and of the faithful came from. Like the logs of a fire, which lose their flame and begin to go out when separated from one another, but which take on new life and heat when brought into contact again, the first Christians came together to rekindle the light and fervor of their faith through sharing and contact with each other around the eucharistic body of Christ.

The essence of Christian community, then, is Eucharist, or the celebration of Christ—of his presence, his life, and his word—by those who have already come to believe. Prior to Eucharist comes evangelization, or the preaching of his word; and prior to this comes pre-evangelization, or those things which make a person willing and able to hear the word.

In the primitive kerygma, or proclamation of the good news of Christ, the typical pattern was pre-evangelization: some incident that shocked, that excited attention and raised questions only the message of faith could answer; then evangelization, in which an apostle got up and explained that only through belief in Jesus Christ could the incident that had just taken place be made intelligible; and finally, after conversion and baptism, came Eucharist, or the celebration together of the reality of the Lord, deeply and personally experienced by all who were present. Pentecost is described in the Acts of the Apostles, for example, as an incident—the apostles' enthusiasm and gift of tongues—which was so inexplicable to the bystanders that they thought the apostles must be drunk. Then Peter got up and explained that this view was rather the fulfillment of the prophecy that said, "I will pour out my Spirit upon all men," a prophecy brought to its realization through Jesus Christ, now risen and Lord. Finally, those who accepted the word and were converted—some three thousand that day—are described as celebrating Eucharist together, spending their time in learning from the apostles, "taking part in the fellowship meals and the prayers" (Acts 2:42).

This was Christian community: its focus was Jesus the Lord; its constitutive element was the common expression and sharing of faith in his Gospel message; and its joy was the joy of the presence of Christ and of his Spirit in the hearts of all.

After the first Christian proclamation, miracles ceased to be the order of the day, and the role of pre-evangelization, of the incident that shocked and excited questions only faith could answer, was supplied by the phenomenon of Eucharist itself. It was the joy, the enthusiasm, and the ring of authenticity of the Christian community's faith that caused disciples to come and look for answers for the preaching of the word. Above all it was the love for God and for one another that so obviously stemmed from this faith, was nourished by faith, and depended on faith for its nature and existence that attested to new disciples that the Spirit was real.

This is not to say there were no dissensions or factions in the early Christian community; the epistles bear eloquent witness that there were. But there was an underlying, strong authenticity to the early Christian's faith that was rooted in the risk all ran together: to be baptized was to be ostracized by the Jews, persecuted by the Romans, and alienated from all the culture of that day. It was evident that a Christian's faith in those days was real, for he professed at the risk of his life. And Jesus said, "Greater love than this no man has, that he lay down his life for his friend." Martyrdom was the criterion, and the daily risk of martyrdom was the experience, of the early Christians' authentic love for Christ.

In a very deep way, then, Christian community was built around a visible phenomenon of martyrdom. It was built around the literal, visible following of Jesus to the cross on the part of some which made real to all the members of the community the fact that each one had already died to this world in Christ and was living for the life to come. The common risk all ran in being Christian was the core of their unity with one another, because it was the one thing that made the solid reality of each one's faith appear.

After persecution had ceased, and Christianity had become the recognized—even the established—religion of the Roman Empire, something was lost. Now Christians no longer recognized in one another a common response of faith that risked this whole world to belong to Christ. People were Christian because that's what everyone was—what else was there to be? Conversions had taken place en masse, through the decision of this or that ruler to accept Christianity himself. When Clovis, king of the Gauls, accepted baptism, we can imagine him lining up his troops and saying, "All right, boys, we're going to be Catholics now. Get into the river! You're being baptized." And when the troops came out of the river we can hear him saying, "Kneel down now! The priest is saying Mass." And from that point on the Mass became not the eucharistic celebration of those for whom belief in Christ was a living, personal reality, but a time for gathering together a horde of half-instructed, semi-pagan Catholic conformists to teach and exhort them to live, externally, at least, in a way not too visibly incompatible with Christian faith and morals. This was not Christian community; it was at most the building of a Christian culture to replace a pagan one. But culture is not religion, and cultural Catholics are not a faith-community.

The Christian response to the disappearance of martyrdom was the flight to the desert. Those who wanted to experience the radicality and unambiguousness of their personal belief went out into the desert where nothing could be drawing them but God. And there, through a visible stance toward this world that renounced any hope in things created, they expressed and experienced the sincerity of their stance in faith toward the invisible reality of the Kingdom of God. The monks replaced the martyrs as the unambiguous sign of the radical risking of Christian faith.

In our day many different things might be said about the contribution of celibates to the local community, but their most important and most fundamental contribution is just to be a sign of the orientation of Christianity toward the invisible mystery and presence of God. They perform other functions. Celibates teach, nurse, bring assistance to the poor and oppressed, and participate in political action to transform social structures in this world. Celibate priests run parishes and schools—and in both capacities complain that their work is mostly administrative, routine administration of the sacraments, or counseling on the human, psychological level. In these "functional" roles, celibacy has no particular significance other than practical. But the real value of celibacy is to be an unambiguous sign, a visible, radical stance taken toward this world through a completely gratuitous renunciation of one of the deepest values of this world, that proclaims in a visible way the invisible presence of grace. Celibacy is a voluntary, unnecessitated risk; it is not called for or demanded by anything other than its own intrinsic value as an act of self-expression. It is something one does purely and simply for what the doing of it expresses.

And this is the key: to express one's faith radically and unambiguously is to experience oneself radically and unambiguously as a believing person. The value of celibacy is simply that, as an abiding, existential gesture, a gesture that invests one's very being in the chosen orientation of one's life, it leaves no doubt about where one has chosen to stand. To the Christian who proclaims, "Christ is my enough," a skeptical voice says, "Prove it." If you believe Christ can really be known and loved—in this world, here and now—in a total, human, personal way, then put your money where your mouth is. Give up every other possibility of the deepest human love in this life; give up marriage. If you find then that you really do develop as a deeply loving person, if you can find joy and deep satisfaction in your relationship with Jesus Christ, if you show signs of loving and being loved instead of the insecurity, defensiveness, and pettiness of a bachelor or old maid, then we will believe (and what is more basic, you yourself will be able to believe) that, yes, Jesus Christ is as real as you say he is.

In the words of Karl Rahner, the value of celibacy simply comes down to this: you don't really know if you believe in the two birds in the bush until you let go of the one bird in the hand. Only in this case Jesus Christ is not a bird in the bush, but an invisible reality in man's heart. The man who wants to experience the real strength and sincerity of his belief that the invisible God is truly in his heart can do so by giving up the visible girl in his arms. In this case he is not professing that human love is bad, or that God is only pleased by renunciation and sacrifice. He is not even saying that to give up the girl is necessarily a "better" way to love Christ. He is only recognizing the fact that by giving up the girl he at least leaves no doubt about the authenticity of his belief in the presence of Christ. There would be no other reason for giving up the girl; it is a pure, symbolic gesture, an act of letting go that attests the sincerity of one's belief in what one already professes to have.

Celibacy, then, like martyrdom or monastic exodus to the desert, is a sign that says something to the whole Christian community about the deepest identity of each individual member. What celibacy expresses is the reality of the Christian community's belief in the real presence of Christ, and of God through grace, to the mind and heart of every Christian. The celibate expresses it in a radical, unambiguous way, like the martyr who literally went to the cross with Christ, or like the monk who went out to the desert. But what the celibate expresses is a part of every Christian's life.

Celibates need lay people—and vice versa. Each reassures the other with regard to what Christianity is all about. The lay vocation makes it very clear that Christianity accepts this world, is committed to redeeming, and not just to leaving behind, the secular realities and structures of this world. The religious vocation, on the other hand, guarantees that this world is not what Christianity is ultimately all about, that the Gospel is a call to transcend this world, to die to the world as such and to live in Christ. But for each state of life to make its contribution to the community, each must live its own vocation radically. The layman must be radically committed to reforming this world, to embodying the truth and values of the Gospel in his own life—in family and in work, and in his use of economic power—at whatever cost to himself. The religious must be one who has visibly and radically renounced all expectations of the good life in this world, at least so far as he himself is concerned.

The temptation exists for each variety of Christian to live the perfectly balanced life—to make use of this world's offerings in a detached but reasonable way, with just the right touch of renunciation to show that one's treasure is in heaven; to be emancipated from this world without breaking with it, and to give one's support to Gospel values in society without total, radical involvement. This is the death of Christian community, because then every person's life expresses equally—and equally obscures—what Christianity is all about. There is no radical witness to anything. There is just the very reasonable, enlightened-appearing mediocrity of a total Christian expression reduced to its lowest common denominator. What this will be in reality is cultural Catholicism—the Gospel of Jesus insofar as the culture of a given time and place is able to understand and accept it. Christianity will appear as simply a little more sharply-focused reflection of the image of natural man, seen in the most representative light of this world, with a little help from above. What will not appear is risk: nobody will stand out as taking any chances based on faith. The "reasonable service" of Christianity will be approved as reasonable—or at least as a fifty-fifty option, given the uncertainty of any values in this world—by believers and non-believers alike. There will be no common realization of having cast one's lot irrevocably, recklessly, with Christ, staking all on the truth of his word, that will make Christians appreciate and depend on one another.

For celibacy to make its contribution to the Christian community, it must stand out as a radical expression of risk, as an integral way of life including not only celibacy

but the prayer and penance, the poverty and total surrender of self, the unambiguous relinquishing of this world,
that religious life has been through the ages. Catholics
must learn to see in their celibate religious not a welcome
supply of volunteer labor for the Church, but a sign and
expression of what Christianity is—of what it is in us all.
What the Christian community must be grateful for is not
the work of celibate religious, but the way of life they live.
The first question Catholics should ask of religious is not
"What do you intend to do in the parish?" but "How do
you intend to live for us?" And religious should realize
that their fundamental role in the Christian community is
to live in such a way that they pose questions to man
which can only be answered by the authentic explanation
of the Gospel of Jesus Christ.

Symbolic gesture is the key to celibacy, and the key to
liturgy, and the key to human love. Lovers express themselves, and their self-expression never stops at words.
When Christians begin to express to themselves and to
one another—just for the sake of expressing it—the depth
and intensity of their faith and love for God, community
will be born. And then perhaps it will be my no-nonsense
cousin who finds himself out in the aisle at Mass, pro-
pelled by something rising joyously within him, to embrace every being in the church.

Notes on the Contributors

L. PATRICK CARROLL, S.J. is an associate pastor in Seattle, Washington, and co-director of the Institute for Spiritual Resources in that city. He is co-author of other books including, *Inviting the Mystic, Supporting the Prophet.*

KEITH CLARK, O.F.M., CAP. is Vicar Provincial for the Midwest Province. Also the author of other books, he is a popular retreat director.

PATRICK J. CONNOLLY is a diocesan priest of the diocese of Gary, Indiana. He is principal of Bishop Noll Institute in Hammond, Indiana.

VIRGINIA SULLIVAN FINN has been active in lay ministry, particularly in the field of learning development. She is affiliated with Weston School of Theology, Cambridge, Massachusetts.

JOHN GARVEY writes regularly for *Commonweal.* In the column "Of Several Minds," he has covered a range of topics from Auschwitz to Atheism to Catholics and Sex. He is author of a book on contemporary spirituality.

226

JOHN F. KAVANAUGH, S.J. is Associate Professor of Philosophy at St. Louis University. He is well known as film critic and author, and is winner of a National Catholic Press Association annual award.

CHRISTOPHER KIESLING, O.P. holds several degrees, one being a S.T.D. from the Pontifical Theological Faculty of Washington, D.C. Both teacher and author, Father Kiesling is also editor of *Spirituality Today.*

DAVID M. KNIGHT, S.J. holds a Ph.D. in theology from the Catholic University of America. Presently, he is Spiritual Director for the Jesuits of Loyola University, New Orleans.

WILLIAM F. KRAFT, Ph.D. is Professor of Psychology at Carlow College in Pittsburgh. A practicing psychotherapist, he is author, lecturer, and director of workshops related to mental health.

KENNETH R. MITCHELL, Ph.D. was Director, Division of Religion and Psychiatry, The Menninger Foundation, Topeka, Kansas. He is now Professor of Pastoral Care, Eden Theological Seminary, Webster Groves, Missouri.

SEBASTIAN MOORE, O.S.B. is a monk of Downside Abbey. A well-known author and lecturer, and formerly on the faculty of Marquette University, he is presently on the faculty of Boston College.

JEROME MURPHY-O'CONNOR, O.P. has been Professor of New Testament at Ecole Biblique in Jerusalem since 1967. A specialist on the Dead Sea Scrolls, he is the author of several books and numerous articles.

HENRI J. M. NOUWEN is a native of Holland where he was ordained to diocesan priesthood in 1957. He has taught at Yale and Notre Dame Universities, and recently has been appointed to the faculty of Harvard Divinity School. His writing and lecturing are widely known.

MARTIN W. PABLE, O.F.M., CAP. is Professor of Theology and the Behavioral Sciences at St. Francis Seminary, Milwaukee. He is well known for his work in and writing on seminary formation.

Annotated Bibliography

Brown, Gabrielle, *The New Celibacy,* N.Y.: Ballantine Books, 1980.

Reflections by a lay woman on why more lay men and women are abstaining from sex and enjoying it. First and last chapters are especially worthwhile.

Gill, James J., S.J., M.D. and Amadeo, Linda, R.N., M.S., "Celibate Anxiety," *Human Development,* 1 (Winter, 1980), 6–17.

A clinical discussion of anxiety and its place in celibates' lives. Addresses the question, "Is there any reason to think that celibates will experience more or less anxiety than non-celibates?"

Gill, James J., S.J., M.D., "Why We See It in Priests," *Medical Insights* (December, 1969), 21–32.

Hoping that marriage will cure their depression, hundreds of priests have left the priesthood. In this interview, James Gill, a priest-psychiatrist, describes such priests and answers the question, "Will marriage solve the problem for these men?"

Kraft, William F., "A Psychospiritual View of Masturbation," *Human Development,* 3 (Summer, 1982), 39–45.

Examines the nature of masturbation and various attitudes toward it. Stresses how critical is the discovery of the underlay of masturbation: feelings of disembodiment, fatigue, loneliness, boredom, and depression. Excellent graphic on p. 42 indicating that the main message of masturbatory acts is that our sexuality and spirituality are not well integrated.

May, Gerald, M.D., Ch. 6, "Relationship: Interpersonal Dynamics in Spiritual Direction," (N.B. "Sexual Feelings in Direction" and "Dealing with Sexuality in Direction"), *Care of Mind Care of Spirit.* Cambridge: Harper and Row Publishers, 1982, pp. 110–122.

Faces a common and natural but seldom addressed situation in spiritual direction. Offers sound clinical/pastoral suggestions *in re.*

McGovern, Joseph D. "Psychosexual Aspects of Maturity—A Developmental Point of View," *Personal Development and Formation,* Washington, D.C.: NCEA, Seminary Department. 1975.

Considers male religious formation in the light of universal laws and principles of psychosexual maturity. Analyzes nine "cases"of psychosexual immaturity, e.g., "frustrated perfectionist," "Machiavellian manipulation," "compulsive-over-achievement." Includes a valuable section about what lessons for formation itself these cases can teach.

Perry, Robert, O.P., *Celibacy: One Expression of Conversion,* NCR Cassette #A 1369, 75 minutes.

A fresh and realistic approach to celibacy, with insights concerning celibacy and the minister's vitality for proclaiming the Gospel.

Peter, Valentine J., "Four Rules for Man—Woman Relationships Among Religious," *Review for Religious,* 41 (March–April, 1982), 207–213.

Discusses widespread uneasiness *re* man–woman relationships among celibates, and need for guidance in them. Proposes four rules conducive to a "strong, positive growth posture" in such relationships.

Rahner, Karl, Ch. 10, "The Celibacy of the Secular Priest Today: An Open Letter," *Servants of the Lord,* N.Y.: Herder and Herder, 1968, pp. 149–172.

A sensitive treatment of the burden, riddle, and challenge of human sexuality as experienced by celibates, specifically secular priests. Supports the position that celibacy is a genuine alternative in Christian life notwithstanding.

Ricoeur, Paul, "Wonder, Eroticism, and Enigma," *Cross Currents,* 14 (Spring, 1964), 133–166.

A classic. Develops the thesis that contemporary problems concerning sexuality arise from depreciation of the concept of the sacred which gave meaning to life and to sexuality. Shows how eroticism becomes an imperative and a revenge in response to disappointments in other sectors of life.

Santos, Gregory, O.C.S.O., "Celibacy, Creativity, and the
   Virgin Archetype," *Chicago Studies,* 21 (Summer,
   1982), 177–189.

Reflections on celibacy in the light of Jungian principles.
Sees the mature celibate as one who creatively transforms
the sexual instinct out of instinctual energy.